ARCHITECTURE STUFF
ROBERT LIVESEY

AF070269

For
Diana
Jessica, Cecilia, Jonathan
Charles, Holden, and Annabel

Published by Applied Research and Design Publishing, an imprint of ORO Editions.
Gordon Goff: Publisher

www.appliedresearchanddesign.com
info@appliedresearchanddesign.com

Architecture Stuff: Copyright © 2020, Knowlton School, The Ohio State University.

All rights reserved. No part of this book may be reproduced, stored in a retrieval system, or transmitted in any form or by any means, including electronic, mechanical, photocopying of microfilming, recording, or otherwise (except that copying permitted by Sections 107 and 108 of the U.S. Copyright Law and except by reviewers for the public press) without written permission from the publisher.

You must not circulate this book in any other binding or cover and you must impose this same condition on any acquirer.

Author: Robert Livesey
Editor: Benjamin Wilke
Book Design: Benjamin Wilke
Project Manager: Jake Anderson

10 9 8 7 6 5 4 3 2 1 First Edition

ISBN: 978-1-951541-02-6

Color Separations and Printing: ORO Group Ltd.
Printed in China.
Typeface: Akzidenz-Grotesk Pro

AR+D Publishing makes a continuous effort to minimize the overall carbon footprint of its publications. As part of this goal, AR+D, in association with Global ReLeaf, arranges to plant trees to replace those used in the manufacturing of the paper produced for its books. Global ReLeaf is an international campaign run by American Forests, one of the world's oldest nonprofit conservation organizations. Global ReLeaf is American Forests' education and action program that helps individuals, organizations, agencies, and corporations improve the local and global environment by planting and caring for trees.

CONTENTS

7   Acknowledgments

8   Foreword by Jeffrey Kipnis

12   Introduction

14   Similarity and Difference:
       SANAA's Grace Farms River Building

30   Shoehorning the Site:
       Koolhaas's Villa Dall'Ava

46   As a Consequence:
       Stirling's Neue Staatsgalerie, Stuttgart

66   Piling It On:
       Vanna Venturi House

86   Primordial Presence:
       Kahn's Kimbell Art Museum

104   Whirring Bits:
       Chareau's Maison de Verre

126   Gulp:
       Hawkmoor's St. George's Bloomsbury

150   Credits

152   Biography

ACKNOWLEDGMENTS

I am afraid that I have been at this so long and have spoken to so many people about this book that I will leave out an incredibly important assistant or influence. I would like to thank the faculty, students, and staff at the Knowlton School for of all their support. I would like to thank Michael Cadwell for his patience and generous financial support. In addition, I would like to thank the students and faculty—Doug Graf, Jackie Gargus, and Jose Oubrerie, in particular—for their constant questioning and for being such great irritants. Todd Gannon was part of this project before he left the Knowlton School and has continued to be a supporter upon his return. I appreciate the good work that my student assistants, Jacqueline Stern, Luke Dougal, and Kevin Jones, provided in producing many of the drawings in *Architecture Stuff*. Thanks to Robert Hintz for providing some of the images for St. George's Bloomsbury. I got a good "pre-read" from Allison Drda, Robert Kahn, and John Rieke, so if the text is difficult to understand, it is their fault. Jeff Kipnis has been a constant inspiration by always coming up with novel ideas. I also very much appreciate Jeff's foreword. Thanks to Gordon Goff and Jake Anderson of ORO for their good work on my behalf. My final praise goes to Ben Wilke. Ben has done it all: revising the text, finding the images, and designing the book. He has been incredibly gracious to put aside his work for the moment to make this book happen.

Looking back at my work, there are many more people to thank. I have listed my co-conspirators with the projects, but, as we know, architecture requires a team. Steven Lesser worked with me on the essay for Maison Truc. Mark Rosenstein helped with the Solow Townhouses and the Baum House. There was a full team from NBBJ for Harold Nester Hall, but Eric Lagerberg was instrumental in its representation and Dimitri Smirniotopoulos headed the contract document team. Lincoln Street Studio produced the working drawings for Warren Street. Todd Gannon made the model for Old Kings Highway. Luke Kautz produced the 3D images for the Town Street Condominiums. A team at Moody Nolan headed by Jon Guldenzopf produced the Northern Kentucky Gateway. Finally, the students at Tianjin University, led by Yun Huang, Siying Li, and Xuerui Wang, produced the drawings for the Fuzhou University Research Building. And of course there are the clients who made the work possible, and to them I am thankful for their indulgences.

FOREWORD By Jeffrey Kipnis

Before I say anything else, I must say this: *Architecture Stuff* is not an easy read, even for someone well versed in reading architectural analysis. That said, I should also say that it is not much more difficult for a beginner with a strong interest in architecture than for a pro. The difficulties arise because Rob Livesey does not aspire simply to "explain" the works he considers. That is, he does not seek to answer the predictable questions that would satisfy the curiosity about the works that might be expected of a reader. Livesey has something very different in mind, far more intriguing and original.

Were I to have been asked to write a cover blurb for Rob Livesey's *Architecture Stuff* rather than these introductory remarks, I would have tendered this:

> I'd stake my reputation that, upon reading Livesey's account of his or her work in these pages, the reaction of the architect would go something like this: "Well, I won't argue his analysis is ingenious as far as it goes, and, true enough, sometimes he even approaches my own thinking, but on balance he fails to grasp my overall concept entirely." And to that plaint I expect Livesey might well respond, "Exactly! It's not that I fail to grasp anything. It's just that I am not so interested in the *Big Idea*."

Exactly. As the readers of *Architecture Stuff* will discover, the fascinations that drive this book are with exquisite episodes and partial relationships more than consummate totalities. Setting aside the original architect's agenda and means, Livesey instead concentrates on his own favorite instances of exceptional architectural play-craft in each work. Nothing makes Livesey's distraction from the original architectural intentions more obvious than the perverse list of projects he considers canonic works by Hawksmoor, Stirling, Koolhaas, SANAA, Venturi, Kahn, and Chareau. Each of these works is already well-recognized within the discipline for the power of its cultural concept and the consummate success of the architectural incarnation. Yet, on the other hand, those seven cultural concepts are, at the very least, discomfited by one another, if not downright antagonistic. Kahn, Koolhaas, and Chareau, aligned? I don't think so. Throw in SANAA??? Fuhgeddaboudit!!!! If each on its own offers a transcendent architectural aria of a worldview, throw them together into the same revue and they make for a lively but chaotic collection of immeubles-vivant, a burlesque in architecture of this unsettled world.

Now, some care must be exercised here, for the point here is **not** to claim that Livesey is blasé about coherent works of architecture whose internal concinnity serves a larger idea. Were that to have been the case, his chosen examples for consideration would likely have been very different. At least since the mid-'60's, a substantial body of important architectural works—ranging from those of established masters such as Rossi, Gehry, and Moss to relative newcomers such as Diller+Scofidio and MOS—have challenged the *bona fides* of the ancient ethos that some palpable sensibility resonates throughout an architectural work and grants it organic unity.

If for millennia the means of achieving such resonance were limited to formal typology or traditional materiality and ornamentation, today the catalog of architectural instruments is immeasurably larger. Advances in building materials, structural systems, and construction methods have dramatically expanded the palette of the architect to be sure, but far more important to the dramatic explosion of design variation in the 20th century has been the emergence of new clienteles for the art form and consequent new audiences for its performances. Today, organic resonance achieved by pictorialism, combinatorial logic, quotation, collage, or allusions augment the venerable catalog of form, materiality, and ornament, as do a dizzying array of other design tactics that range from familiar to exotic to esoteric.

In this volume, Koolhaas (OMA) and SANAA, two architectural practices with close affinities, provide stark evidence as one compares the drama of differences between Grace Farms and Villa dall'Ava, divided by only 20 years, and then, in turn, compare these to Hawksmoor's struggle in form and material in an attempt to unite disparate architectural liturgical types three centuries earlier. Thus, it is hard to image how—or why—one would want to consider them in any other way?

If at first Livesey's analysis of Grace Farms seems almost too dutiful in its deference to the instructions of the building offered by SANAA architect Ryue Nishizawa to attend the landscape as the generator (though do not be fooled, close attention to Livesey's brief discussion lands on at least one issue that neither the architect nor any other critic bother to consider!), by the next work, Koolhaas's Villa dall'Ava, the excursion from the architect's own account and the accumulated critical literature of exegesis could not be more dramatic. Where others see quotation, collage, the dissolution of the nuclear family union, the glorification of mechanicals (sliding doors), and ironic games with urban versus rural/pastoral tropes (e.g., construction fences and swimming pools versus rooftop gardens), Livesey sees only two elements: "walls" and a garden.

To demonstrate just how far Livesey strays in his Koolhaas analysis from the norm, allow me to call attention to but one subtlety that scents Livesey's argument, one apparent gaff that that might easily be missed or even misunderstood as a serious error. He references only Mies van der Rohe and Le Corbusier as the work's predecessors. Philip Johnson is omitted entirely, even though the Johnson Glass House is the most completely quoted element in the Villa dall'Ava; it sticks out like a sore thumb. If, as is standard today, one considers Corb's Villa Savoye, Mies's Farnsworth House, and

Johnson's Glass House as dall'Ava's trio of precedents—leading to a very easy case for a collage argument and Koolhaas swerve to the urban and mechanical—then something is very wrong with Livesey's omission. On the other hand, if one wants to push attention away from that obvious collage reading toward, well, gardens and walls, then the superior antecedents of the Villa are better conceived of as Le Corbusier's Maisons Jaoul (a giant wall!) and Mies's Resor House, whose dumbbell symmetry and inside/outside-space/garden relationship is made thematic explicitly. Hence, for Livesey's analyses, these are the only two influences, and, though it is essential that he note a heritage by naming the two architects, it is just as important that he not identify them as images or tropes.

That is why, to grasp the full force of Livesey's arguments, the opposite is true: he requires the works he takes on to maintain full allegiance to the tradition of the organic whole. This is because he himself is committed to it, but also because his goal in this book is **not** to give us deeper insights into these particular works (as a historian or critic might desire), even if his analyses do offer original interpretations. In my opinion, the ambition and struggle of this volume is toward a worthier, more liberating ambition: to give us deeper insights into how he, as an architect, thinks about his discipline and designs new works. One senses that in this ambition a conviction that *Architecture Stuff* strives to broach a more honest, general, non-verbal model for how most—if not all—architects work, a model whose generative capacity and history of success suggests that it deserves to be elevated to the status of a theory in its own right, even if such a position struggles to be told.

In the end, the greater consequence of Livesey's exercise is to make a compelling if personal case for revisiting the idea of an **independent** architectural intelligence, one that is neither autonomous and independent of external influences, nor best understood in terms of history, theory, criticism, structural engineering, or material sciences, though these and other disciplines are always implicated in that intelligence, just as science, history, and grammar are always implicated in philosophy. What else, after all, could Nietzsche have meant when he wrote, "I fear we are not rid of God, because we still have faith in grammar."

His declaration of independence revives and updates a radical proposition, almost sotto voce, that the "brains" behind this distinct type of intelligence are to be found wholly in an **architectural eye**, here understood not as a metonymy, but as an actuality: a specially evolved and trained bodily organ complex (which would likely need to include eyes, hands, skin, and legs at least) that bypasses, almost as an instinct, the traditionally understood path of artistic apprehension: that is, one that would first see like a camera and then report that sensation to the brain for verbal understanding and later to the mind for interpretation.

It is a radical proposition to be sure, but not as ridiculous as one might think. In the great writings on art, one finds more or less explicit allusions to it in Spinoza, Nietzsche, and Bergson. The great French philosopher Gilles Deleuze took it seriously enough to suggest a grounding of it at a biological level in his writings on the painter Francis Bacon.

And Livesey himself gives us a small clue—so small that I suspect many will miss its significance—that this notion of an *architectural eye*, however one may want to name it, is not just my hysterical concoction as an interpretation of his work, but is indeed, in some sense or another, the very desire he wishes to express in this work, the one that causes it to come into existence and colors its every page.

In Livesey's own introduction, there is a brief mention of the now obscure but once-renowned 19th-century art theorist Konrad Fiedler. To my great embarrassment of ignorance and great joy of discovery, until I read the name in this text, I had never heard of him; he is almost never mentioned by art writers or philosophers who, I now believe, should celebrate his work today. It is understandable that Livesey would want to reference him, because Fiedler first put forth the notion of Pure Visibility in which the entire content of a work of art was grasped in its seeing. Obviously, the idea is very similar in rudimentary form to the implication of Livesey's conjecture today, though the latter is far more provocative and livelier than that of his predecessor.

Which, therefore, is why the conclusion in the form of *More Stuff* is so central to the argument. Though separated from the main text and analyses like chaff from grain and styled as a mere pamphlet appendix or apologetic afterthought, it is, in fact, the climax of the work. For in these few select projects by Livesey, we see a consummate demonstration of the principle of the architectural eye engaged in production. Each project is made of the very same stuff that he has carved out of the masterworks he has analyzed, yet not one is made of any part of them or any other easily recognizable episode.

At the beginning I warned: *Architecture Stuff* is not an easy read. Now you know why. How could it be, when its very message is that what must be grasped is essentially non-verbal! Yet, as one who is nothing but verbal, I offer this assurance: reading it, working through its diagrams and analyses is worth the effort. Doing so with care and close attention is to make an investment of hours that will engender a growth in architectural intelligence for both readers of architecture and producers of architecture that will yield returns for years.

INTRODUCTION

This book is about architecture stuff.

Architecture Stuff has to do with being curious about why things are the way that they are, as in, "What is this stuff?" It also has to do with projecting possibilities, as in, "What can we do with this stuff?" More a working method than a theory, *Architecture Stuff* deals with questions that are pertinent to designers as well as critics of buildings. It deploys observation, interpretation, and invention in equal measure in order to produce a palpable density of ideas.

When it first entered the English language in the 14th century as a noun, *stuff* referred to the quilted material worn under chain mail. Soon after, it came to be associated with equipment and furniture. As a verb, this word derives from an older word, *stuffen*, meaning "to furnish, supply, or cram." This history is useful in unpacking the term. *Architecture Stuff* is concerned with material that resides below the surface and points to the more malleable organizational underpinnings of the discipline. The resonance of the term with equipment and furniture relates to a focus on architecture's discrete elements and components, while *stuffing* aligns with seeing architecture as a dense fabric of relationships produced through transitive action and inventive embellishment.

In a disciplinary context as crammed with jargon as architecture is, some might quibble with the informality of architecture stuff, but such a perceived casualness is important for several reasons. Architecture stuff is unpretentious, accessible, contemporary, and sometimes humorous. It suggests variety and quantity, but not opulence. In the best cases each element is in several relationships at the same time; hierarchy is variable and fluid. Architecture stuff is not an attempt to suggest a lack of disciplinary focus or dearth of authenticity, but to point out the fact that a degree of play is in effect. An important aspect of stuff is that it generalizes. Action can be related to elements; experience is the same as space. Whatever is found or collected in a bedside drawer is fair game.

Architecture stuff is fueled by looking at things: the more you see, the more you get. It can be applied to any building. Architecture stuff is not particularly interested in narrative or storytelling; it is concerned with consequences. If *this*, then *what*? The game of consequences—both logical and illogical—comes from Konrad Fiedler's idea of perceptual cognition, where certain forms of understanding are only visual.

As such, architecture stuff is a particular way of looking at architecture. Economy of gesture (more stuffed into less) is important. Architecture stuff addresses the mundane and is not afraid of the literal. It is anti-branding and anti-fetish. It allows for specificity without certainty. It encourages the episodic and eclectic and embraces humor as a way of not taking itself too seriously. By necessity it is fixed, but its stasis is fleeting.

Rather than rehearse tired dichotomies between form and space or object buildings and urban fabric, architecture stuff operates beneath the fray rather than above it. As others today debate architecture's politics (see criticality), ethics (see sustainability), and technical potentialities (see digital processes and fabriaction), architecture stuff attends to that which is irreducibly disciplinary. Politics, ethics, and technology—however important—cannot make architecture by themselves. More stuff is required.

As the story goes, the industrial revolution killed the craft of architecture in order to give the multitude plenty. Today, some architects and designers promise a facsimile of lost craft with endless scripted variations. But the pleasure of craft does not lie in the elements themselves; the pleasure of craft emerges from the density of the relationships within and among the parts being used. Mass produced variation is a bore.

Architecture Stuff demonstrates other ways to access the pleasures of craft. It sanctions the promiscuousness and invention that exist in the making of relationships. It welcomes the marriage of one-off customization with off-the-shelf componentry. It knits disparate elements together without reducing their inherent complexities and it unravels familiar configurations in favor of novel organizational possibilities. Architecture stuff counters the empty veneer of blindly fabricated variation by exposing a profuse depth of relationships within any building, and here considers examples by Nicholas Hawksmoor, Pierre Chareau, Louis Kahn, Robert Venturi, James Stirling, Rem Koolhaas, and SANAA. These buildings are not chosen for their allegiance to any stylistic or ideological categorization, but for their demonstrable intelligence, density of detail, and wit. In other words, they are chosen for their breadth of architectural approaches and because they are good examples of architecture stuff.

Fig. 1

14 ARCHITECTURE STUFF

SIMILARITY AND DIFFERENCE:
SANAA'S GRACE FARMS RIVER BUILDING

"Ideas are to objects as constellations are to stars."

- Walter Benjamin

Grace Farms is a cultural community center in New Canaan, Connecticut that focuses on the development of five topics: nature, the arts, justice, community, and faith. Located on 80 acres, the project was designed by SANAA and completed in 2015. The main building is known as the River building because of its meandering serpentine form and reflective roof; it is 1,400 linear feet of splendor that descends more than 40 feet down a hill. (Fig. 1) The River building has five glass pavilions: an auditorium that doubles as a sanctuary, a library, a dining hall, a tearoom, and a gymnasium that can be used for performances. It is SANAA's third building in the United States and by far the best detailed.

According to Ryue Nishizawa, we should pay attention to the integration of architecture and landscape. For him, a building's interior is different than its exterior, as the interior belongs to the inhabitants while the exterior addresses the city. He attempts to erase that distinction by making a landscape-like architecture. He is emphatic that a building cannot be fully understood from one visit or a single view; it must be understood over time. Further, he makes a distinction between Western Architecture and Asian Architecture. The former is more object-oriented; it is solid and additive. The latter is phenomenological; it is experiential and integrated with nature.

The River building is spread out. (Fig. 2) An encompassing roof makes the building singular, but the spaces between the pavilions are vast. By comparison, SANAA's other buildings are compact. Clearly there is a statement being made about the differences between the density of Japan and that of the American suburbs. Although the building has a rambling form, its placement on the site is precise. There are two sets of pre-existing corrals immediately adjacent to the building and it is clear that the building has been composed in relation to them. (Fig. 3) The auditorium is sited north of the western corrals but overlaps the corral grid east-to-west. The same condition is true at the opposite end of the building, where the gymnasium is sited south of the eastern corrals but overlaps them in a similar manner. Both end pavilions are on the same orthogonal grid as the corrals, anchoring themselves and the building to the existing context.

One of the salient aspects of the site is its slope. The building follows the contours of the hill. Like the corral fences, the roof and its rail-like fascia remain a constant height from the ground. However, the volumes of the occupied spaces are allowed to vary. (Fig. 4) In the auditorium, the hill provides a sloped floor while in the gymnasium the recessed floor allows for a double-height space. The 40-foot drop along the length of the building allows for a sectional separation of the pavilions, with 40 feet being the approximate equivalent of a three-story building. The auditorium sits 20 feet or more above the library and the dining pavilion. The dining pavilion sits 10 feet or more above the tearoom and gymnasium pavilions. The River building is both continuous and stacked.

Fig. 2

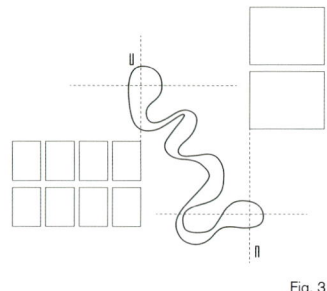

Fig. 3

The slimness of the architectural elements is an important aspect of SANAA's work. In the River building, the fascia of the roof and the diameter of the columns are notoriously thin, and the form of the roof is like a wad of gum that has been stretched to create several areas where the canopy is markedly slim. The thinness is a type of minimalism that is at once a new structural expression, anti-consumerist, anti-Metabolist, and fashion-focused. SANAA has to be given some credit for making a statement that is technical, political, historical, and cultural. It is a case of exaggeration-as-formal-device that allows extreme abstraction to be read in multiple ways.

The transparency of the public pavilions is also readily apparent. Like many other projects by SANAA, the glass allows for superimposed images made up of that which is seen *through* the glass and the reflections seen *on* the glass. In the River building, the reversal exists with respect to how transparent elements might normally be considered. Here, the glass pavilions are used to support the roof (Fig. 5) while the opaque service pavilions float under the roof, eschewing structural support. (Fig. 6) The glass pavilions are lined with a white perimeter steel beam behind the glass. The columns underneath are evenly spaced but are not in the same rhythm as the wood beams above, clearly indicating that it is the pavilion as a whole (rather than any of

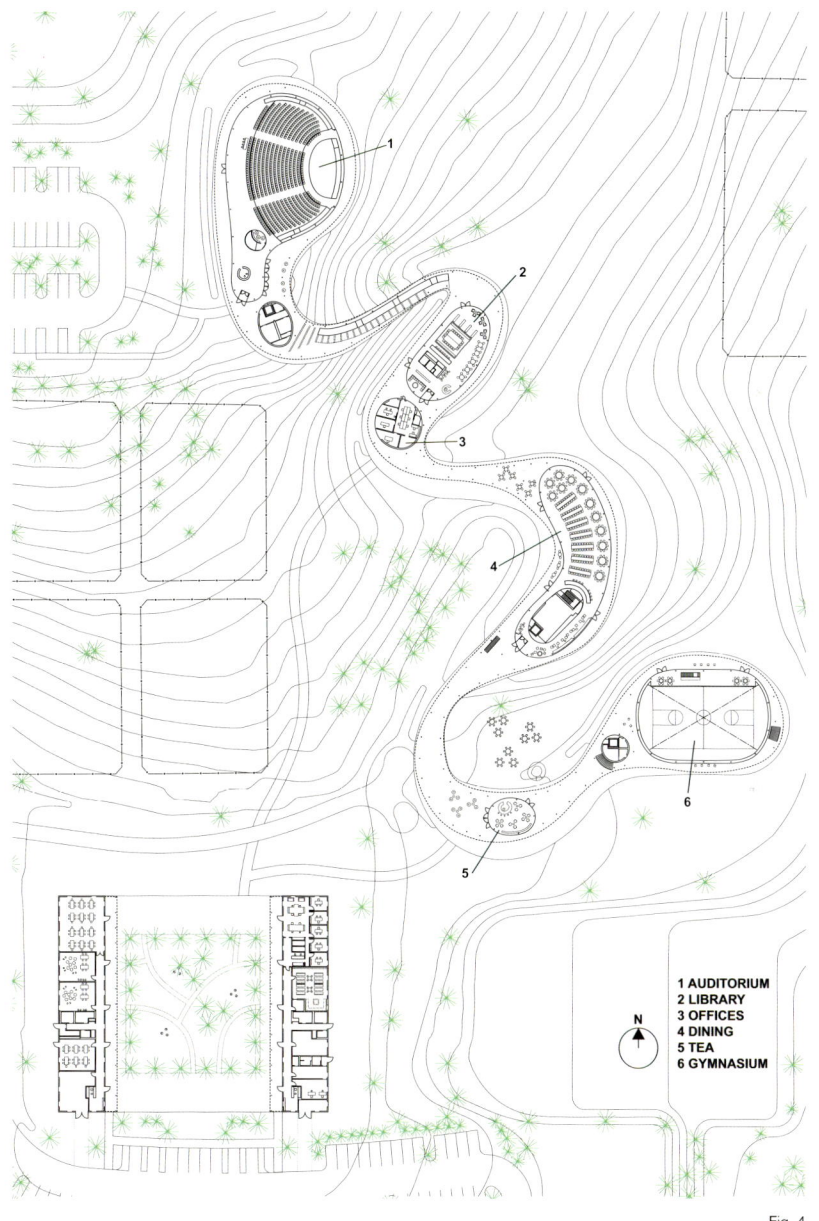

Fig. 4

SIMILARITY AND DIFFERENCE

its singular elements) that supports the roof. In contrast, the opaque service pavilions are separated from the roof by a thick reveal; the solid walls are mere enclosure rather than support. The thin freestanding columns that support the roof stop at the glass pavilions yet run past the opaque pavilions to provide the necessary support.

Fig. 5

Fig. 6

In the pavilions, the lack of registration between the columns and the wood crossbeams might be understood as a mistake, but in fact is a clarification of elements that allows for an elaboration of effects. Given the precision of the individual elements (or systems of elements), the misalignments can only be understood as an articulation to allow for multiple readings. The lack of registration is most clear in the offset of the epoxy river stone path and its relation to the roof above. (Fig. 7) Both undulate in and out, but always to a slightly different rhythm. Another lack of registration can be seen in the fixed linear tables in the dining pavilion that, while evenly-spaced, march to their own rhythm. Sometimes the tables are centered between the beams above and sometimes they are centered on the beams. The difference is made particularly clear because of the presence of the hanging lights that reiterate the beam module. If one understands the spacing of the beams as a bay, the tables are spaced at 1.5 bays and the pavilion columns are typically spaced at 2.5 bays. (Fig. 8)

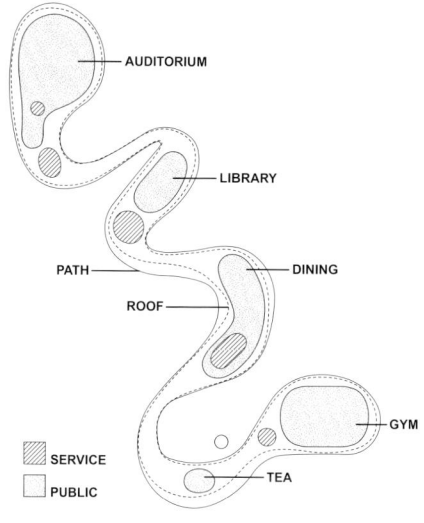

Fig. 7

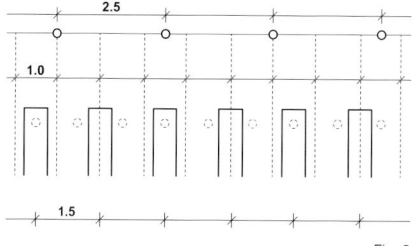

Fig. 8

There are five service pavilions to match the five public pavilions (see Fig. 7), but there is not a one-to-one correspondence. The auditorium has both a quiet room for children within it and a restroom and elevator pavilion just outside. The elevator provides access to the green room and support spaces on the lower level. A private office pavilion is paired with the library, next to and independent of it. The dining pavilion swallows the kitchen service pavilion. The tearoom has no service equivalent but there is a nascent circular pavilion in the form of a barbeque pit adjacent to it. The gymnasium pavilion, like the auditorium pavilion, has a restroom and elevator service pavilion immediately outside of it. These two big pavilions are at either end, as if they are parents protecting their young. One might understand the auditorium as the mother, with a projection that births the intermediate pavilions. In such a scenario, the children's quiet room could be understood as still in the womb.

There is a relentless curvilinear geometry at work in the River building. Everything seems to be curved, from the pavilions themselves to the columns that support the roof; from the reception desks to the easy chairs and round tables; from the pools of light to the scuppers and rain basins; from the myriad lighting fixtures to the air vents in the gymnasium and auditorium; from the tile in the bathrooms to the exit lights on the stairs. Yet, it is not quite that simple; the orthogonal is also ever-present. On the site, the rambling building is framed by the rectangular corrals. In addition to the orientation of the two end pavilions, the two dispersed exit stairs from the lower level of both the auditorium and the gymnasium reiterate the orthogonal geometry of the corrals. (see Fig. 3) In the service pavilions, the rooms are cut from orthogonal geometries and are inserted into the rounded forms. In the library, the conference room, kitchen, and restrooms establish an orthogonal relative to the pavilion; in the gymnasium, the basketball court reiterates the geometry of the corrals. (Fig. 9)

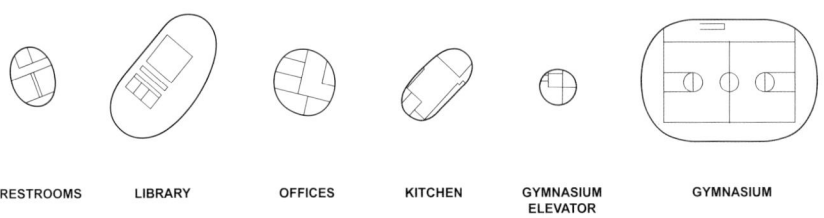

RESTROOMS   LIBRARY   OFFICES   KITCHEN   GYMNASIUM ELEVATOR   GYMNASIUM

Fig. 9

The wrestling match between the orthogonal and curvilinear geometries is most clear in the overall composition of the building. The roof is a meandering linear figure with wide and thin sections. The exposed wood beams in the glass pavilions track the linear form of the building as they span the serpentine form in regular intervals as it steps down the hill. (Fig. 10) On top of the roof, the metal panels do not follow the form of the building; they are linear strips that are set at approximately 45 degrees to the Cartesian grid of the site. Viewed from above, this pattern makes it seem as if the building form had been cut out of lined paper. (Fig. 11) Yet again, SANAA is giving two diametrically opposed interpretations of an element of the building. It may seem peculiar that three exhaust vents puncture the pristine metal rain screen. Yet, if one understands the joints between the metal panels as analogous to the raked gravel in a Zen garden, then the vents might be understood as the rocks that populate it.

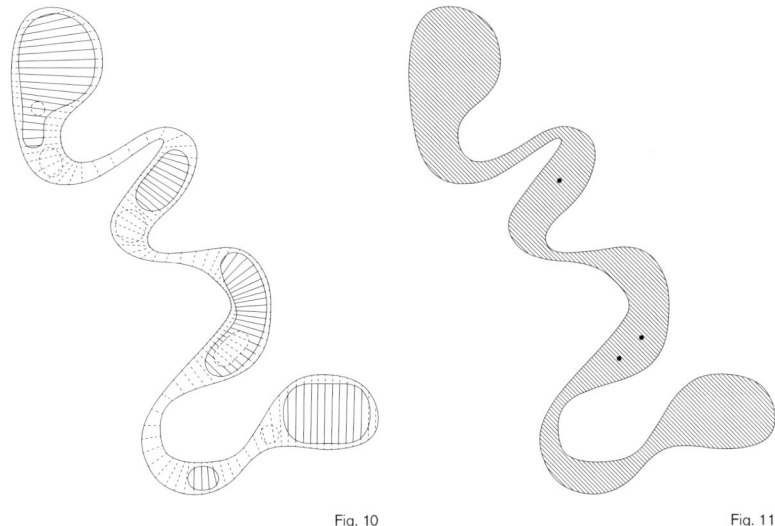

Fig. 10　　　　　　　　　　　　Fig. 11

The soffit of the encompassing roof outside the pavilions is made of boards that run in the same direction as the linear building and span from one structural element to the next. The soffit is bare; nothing is allowed to intrude on the floating plane. It is lit by a line of lights on the ground. (Fig. 12) Inside the pavilions, the boards seem to have been peeled back or pushed up to reveal the wooden structural beams and ceiling elements. Only the inhabited spaces are allowed to puncture the plane, making clear the rare distinction between inside and out.

For SANAA, systems are organized elements. Sometimes it is the consistent rhythm of the elements that is important and sometimes it is the elements themselves. In the pavilions, the distance between columns that hold up the white perimeter beam is constant and made apparent by the modulation of three glass panels between the columns. However, the columns themselves vary in diameter. Clearly the rhythm of the columns is more important than the individual artifacts. The reverse is true with the exposed-wood roof beams in the pavilions. Here the elements are exactly the same size but have to deal with radically different spans. In the auditorium and gymnasium pavilions, the respective 100-foot and 80-foot spans are achieved by adding white steel cables and vertical struts that allow the wood beams to remain constant while creating a truss to achieve the greater spans. (Figs. 13 & 14) As a further elaboration, it is interesting to note the double strut of the auditorium versus the single strut of the gym.

Fig. 12

Fig. 13

Fig. 14

The idea of conjugation is thematic in SANAA's work. The lights at Grace Farms are a good example. There are four essential types: recessed, exposed can, ellipsoid, and tubular. The recessed lights are most evident in the gymnasium (see Fig. 14), though they also exist in a reduced form in the ceiling of the tearoom and in all of the service spaces. In even further-reduced form, the recessed lights are manifest in the up-lights of the paving below the roof (see Fig. 12) and act as emergency exit lights in the risers of the exterior fire stairs. In the auditorium, cans hang from the ceiling to provide the primary lighting. (see Fig. 13) Those cans are found again as track lighting in the library and on the columns at several points along the walkway, providing pools of light for pavilion entrances and clusters of outdoor furniture. The ellipsoid lights provide the primary lighting for the dining hall as chandeliers that hang from the ceiling, but they can also be found as standard lights in the library, tearoom, and sitting area of the dining pavilion. The tubular lights have the same form as the track lighting in the library but are found as circles that define a separate dining area (Fig. 15) and as the lighting source for the reflective *Double Glass River* installation by Teresita Fernández. (Fig. 16)

The River building appears to be a simple edifice. It is a canopy supported by thin columns that follows the contours of a site while sheltering a series of pavilions. The fact that it is made of a limited palette of materials contributes to its singular image, but it is how those materials are layered to appear and disappear with respect to one another that creates a wide range of experiences. The structure aligned with the glass wall is a constant in the public pavilions. In the auditorium and library, curtains are added to allow for the control of lighting levels. The ceilings of the auditorium and gymnasium exist in contrast to one another. The ceiling of the auditorium is cacophonous with its double-strut truss, hanging can lights, and circular bars for stage lights (see Fig. 13), while the ceiling for the gymnasium is more sedate with its single-strut truss and recessed lights. (see Fig. 14) The material palette for the floors is equally selective. In the auditorium, the primary floor is concrete and the stage is wood. In the gymnasium, the primary floor is wood and the gallery floor is concrete. The other pavilions follow suit, with the library floor finished in wood and the restaurant finished in concrete. There are two anomalies in the pattern: the sitting area in the dining pavilion is finished in stone pavers and the tearoom is carpeted. Each material has a particular effect on the character of its respective space.

Fig. 15

Fig. 16

The form of the building makes it seemingly difficult to recognize a proper front or back, with the projections and insets of the building forming a rather ambidextrous whole. Clearly there are sides, with the parking to the west and views down the hill to the east. An additional indication of sidedness is the use of up-lights in the paving that begin at the northwest end of the auditorium pavilion, wrap down the west side of the building, move down the stairs and behind the library west of the office pavilion and the dining hall, continue south of the tearoom, and end on the north side of the gymnasium. (Fig. 17) The lights function as an indicator of the linear arrangement of the building, a path to be followed, a marker of the difference between the two sides, and as an edge to the pavilions and their exterior spaces. With the auditorium, the lights are on the uphill side and behind the seats that face a distant view of the property. With the library, the lights reinforce the backdrop of the service rooms within. For the dining pavilion, the lights reiterate the constricted nature of the one side versus the expansive nature of the other. For the tearoom, the lights tie the pavilion to the adjacent inset space. For the gymnasium—similar to the auditorium—the lights make an edge to the pavilion and its adjacent athletic fields by lining the upper gallery.

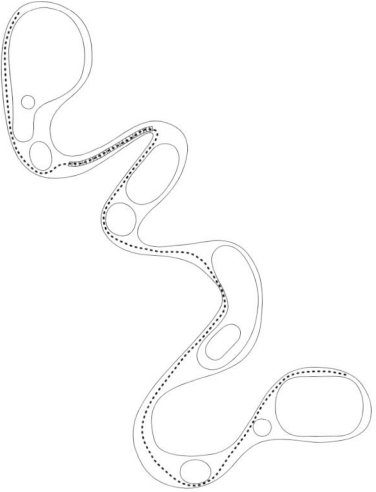

Fig. 17

The views to and from the pavilions define another aspect of sidedness. (Fig. 18) The auditorium is directional with the arrangement of the seats and the sloped floor. From the uphill side, one looks through the pavilion to the fields beyond. The library is similar—but more emphatic—due to the presence of the conference room, service area, restrooms, and a steeply-raked hill that block any view to the northwest. The dining pavilion sits on a ridge with views east and west. The tearoom looks out both north and south, but the view to the north is much more contained by one of the inset courtyards of the building. The glass walls in the gym act as clerestories since the gym floor is a level below grade; there might be sky views, but the real view is into the gym below. Expansive views, near views, through views, intimate views, and inside views use similar glass walls but yield vastly different effects.

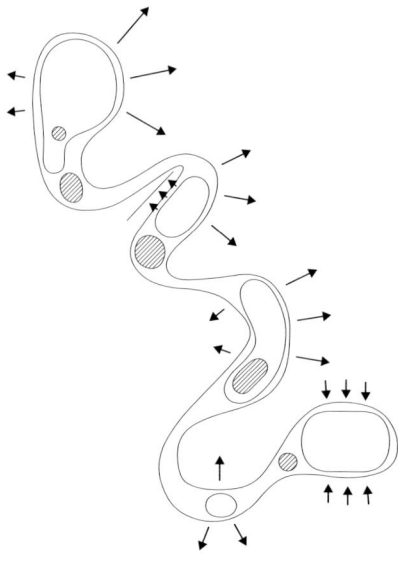

Fig.18

The projections and insets of the building are also elaborated. (Fig. 19) The projection of the auditorium to the east provides the expansive views; its elongated west side allows for an entrance facade from the upper parking lot. The projection of the library to the east is extreme but ultimately only for outdoor reading. The projection of the office pavilion westward aligns with the covered walkway to the south, creating a grand hollowed court with trees. The projection of the dining hall on the ridge is subtle but made effective by pushing the pavilion into the landscape on the east while helping to create the captured grove of trees on the west. The tearoom is a minor player in the projection of the canopy toward the horse barns. Finally, the gymnasium is a projected head, but is primarily oriented to the fields on the south. For all the similarity of the gestures, the experiences are again remarkably different.

For the insets, the two that face west are diametrically opposed. The uphill inset is a sliver of space that is full of topography. From the library, the inset is a wall of plants. (Fig. 20) The second inset adjacent to the dining pavilion is really a bowl with a small grove of trees. (Fig. 21) As viewed from the dining hall, it serves as a contained landscape in contrast to the opposite side that offers an expansive view. On the east side, the uppermost cut primarily provides spacing for views from the auditorium. The second cut is the foreground for the view from the library. The third cut is the deepest and most radical, with the dining and gymnasium pavilions pushing in and leaving an almost completely enclosed courtyard adjacent to the tearoom. (Fig. 22) However, unlike the presence of the dining room on its primary cut, the tearoom is merely an element along the edge of the cut. Conditions are again elaborated in order to provide for very different experiences: deep cut versus shallow cut, open condition versus closed condition, steep hill versus rolling hill, symmetry versus asymmetry, pavilion versus walkway.

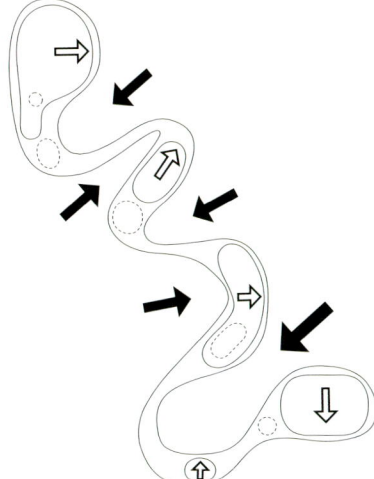

Fig. 19

Fig. 20

SIMILARITY AND DIFFERENCE 27

Fig. 21

Fig. 22

Critics have frequently cited the self-referential nature of SANAA's forms. There are several aspects to the development of such forms as seen in the elaborate and thematic vocabulary. In the River building, there is little doubt that an interest in the biomorphic is a strong component of the form-making. It is pervasive, from the overall figure of the building to the river stones of the paving. As much as the project may be about representing nature, it is just as much about integration with nature. The clarity of the forms is enhanced by their juxtaposition with the Cartesian organization of the existing corrals and stables on the site. Given SANAA's interest in abstraction, juxtaposition is certainly an effective device for giving clarity to forms. In addition to the curvilinear and the orthogonal, strategic juxtapositions are found in the use of solids and voids, fat and thin, insets and projections, and in material realities like the hard reflective steel roof and the soft absorptive wood soffit.

What is important about SANAA's work—and the River building in particular—is the ability to expand the range of applications and consequent experiences with a limited palette of materials and forms. Minimalism is not a simplification, but a densification of attributes. It is an economy of gesture where each element or action produces numerous effects. SANAA is able to generalize the attributes of an auditorium, library, restaurant, tearoom, and gymnasium in such a way that the elements become intimately related without losing their individual character. The limited palette allows for widely divergent experiences for users while blending into a coherent whole.

Fig. 1

SHOEHORNING THE SITE:
KOOLHAAS'S VILLA DALL'AVA

"The action of its presence modifies minds, each according to its nature and state, provoking combinations latent within a certain head, but whatever reaction is thus produced, the text is found to be unaltered and capable of indefinitely generating other phenomena in other circumstances or in another person."

- Paul Valéry

Villa dall'Ava is classic Wizard of Oz: it's all thunder and lightning behind that wall. (Fig. 1) There are at least seven overlapping themes that occur throughout the house. First is the definition of *suburban* as a conjunction of city and country estate. Second is the deployment of modernist quotes, specifically of Mies van der Rohe and Le Corbusier. Third is the development of an architectural vocabulary whose elements are defined in relationship to one another. Fourth is what one might refer to as *action architecture*, where all elements have been acted upon by being compressed, stretched, slipped, or repeated. Fifth is a modernist interpretation of symmetry or the transformation of an *A-B-A* organizational scheme into an *S* diagram. Sixth is a riff on layering. Finally, there is the materiality of the building that is at once luscious and cheap looking.

The stories begin in the driveway. (Fig. 2) Asphalted and compressed between the massive concrete house wall and the raised and corseted v-shaped garden wall of

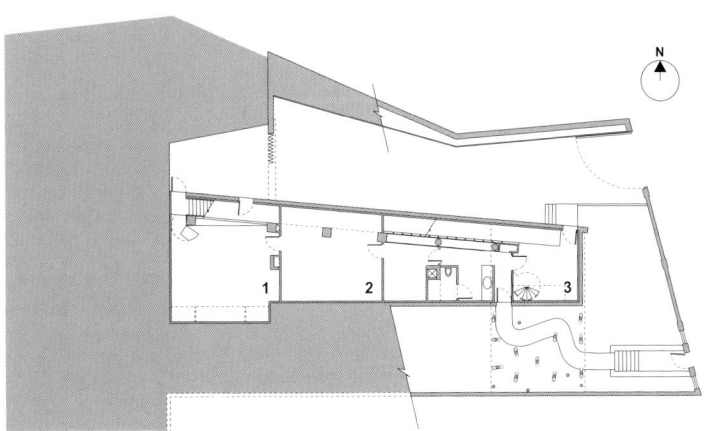

1. LIBRARY 2. STORAGE 3. FRONT HALL   Fig. 2

the neighbor to the north, the driveway is an extension of the city. The neighbor's wall pushes the massive concrete wall to the side, revealing the back pavilion. Not unlike the Parthenon as seen from the Propelea, the angle of the concrete wall provides the full effect of its presence: three stories of concrete sliced by a full-story glass loggia. (see Fig. 1)

Surrounded by garden on three sides, Koolhaas pulls some if it down alongside the driveway, thus completing a full wrap of the site and setting a city-country combination on a suburban lot. (Fig. 3) This adds to the already compressed (with at least a 5-to-1 aspect ratio) side garden behind the house wall that is orthogonally aligned with the southern neighbor's garden wall. (Fig. 4)

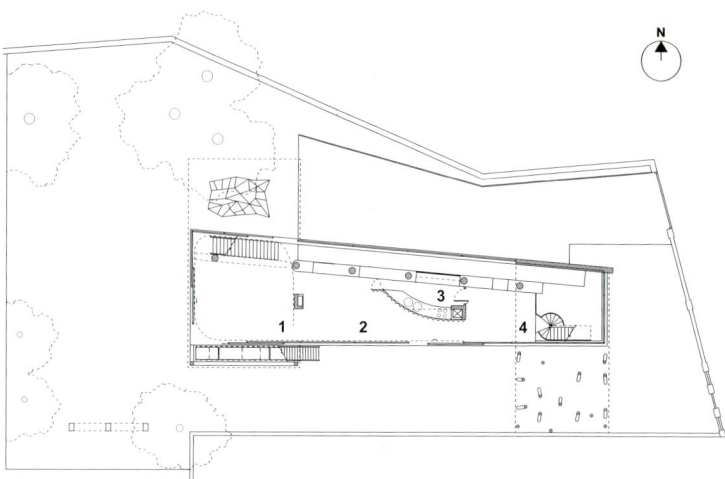

1. LIVING 2. STUDY 3. KITCHEN 4. DINING

Fig. 3

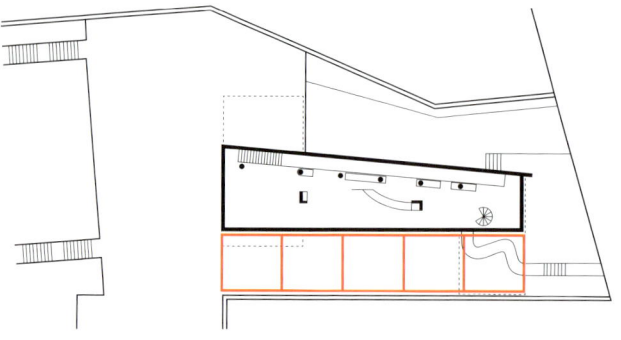

Fig. 4

The house has two front elevations (that face the driveway and the street) and two back elevations (Figs. 5 & 6) (that face the side garden and the rear uphill garden). Both front elevations are urban; both rear elevations relate to the country. The driveway elevation is big and bold. The side garden elevation is endlessly differentiated and layered top-to-bottom with elevated pavilions at each end. The street and uphill garden elevations are primarily the two pavilions. The street-facing pavilion is contingent and contextual. The uphill garden-facing pavilion floats as an object in the backyard. Seen from the street, the angled concrete wall sets up a perspective trick: the rear pavilion is larger but further away while the street pavilion is smaller and closer. The rear pavilion allows for a certain largess while the front pavilion is situated where space is at a premium and where it is further reduced by the impact of the concrete wall. This condition can be read from the street (see Fig. 1) and in plan. (Fig. 7) Even the glass panels on the piano nobile are scaled to fit. (Fig. 8)

Fig. 5

Fig. 6

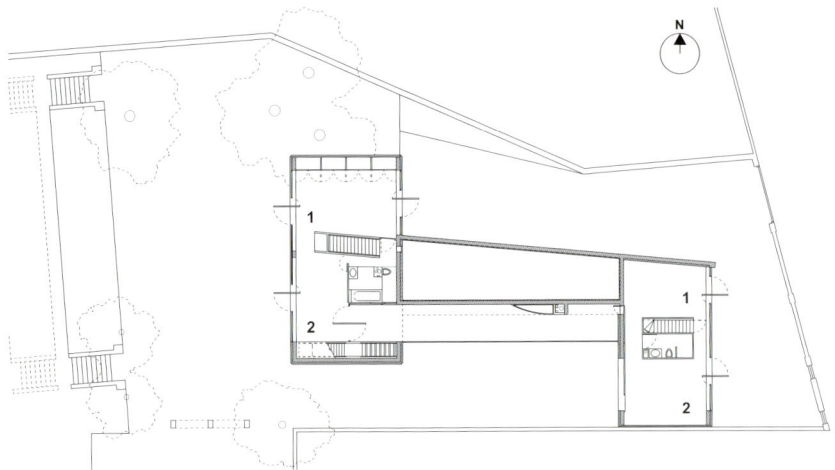

1. BEDROOM 2. STUDY

Fig. 7

Fig. 8

The house wall is actually a garden wall turned back on itself. (Fig. 9) Its status as a garden wall is made apparent by the fact that it juts past the house that it fronts. The door-in-the-wall in the northeast corner reiterates the scale of a garden wall and provides access to a walled interior garden/entrance hall. The metal underside of the pavilion above, the green terrzzo floor, and the circular steel stair (Fig. 10) with its "bough" leading to the second floor all indicate that we are in a garden that is somewhat familiar and slightly foreign. Hints that the "real" ground is at the first floor include the "falling" wood wall along the ramp (Fig. 11) and the common green terrazzo floor of the living level and the entrance hall. A third clue is at the roof where the concrete wall has kept a slice of the earth in place as the rest has fallen away to reveal the geological layers. Within this interpretation, the stone wall that is adjacent to the side garden is just a rock layer and the glass piano nobile is the revealed underground river. (see Fig. 8)

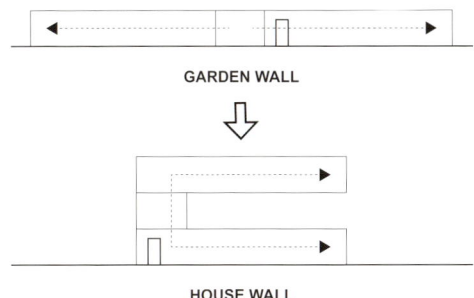

Fig. 9

Fig. 10

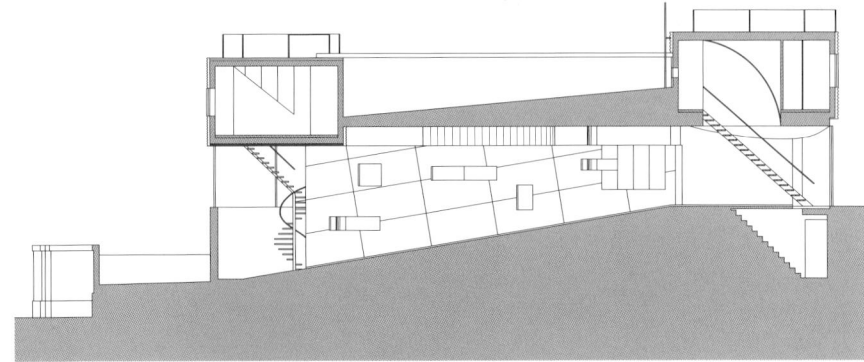

Fig. 11

There are other indications of the tensions and differences between Villa Dall'Ava as a house in the city and a house in the country. The front corrugated box pavilion is hung off the concrete wall. Though this box is fully frontal with respect to the street, the concrete wall pushes into it. As part of the city, the elevated pavilion fills the limited space by being pushed toward the south neighbor and the property line that divides the two. As part of the country, the front pavilion is like its twin counterpart in the back, floating above and in the garden. (see Fig. 1) The driveway steps also work to reveal the differences between city and country, as they are pushed tight against the house between the driveway and the concrete wall; as a counterpoint, the steps in the garden are allowed to float freely at the end of the meandering path. (see Fig. 2)

In the garden, there is a multitude of elements working simultaneously. The rear pavilion is clearly a modernist box that floats above the ground below, recalling the gate-keeper's house at Villa Savoye. (see Fig. 6) Due to its grand scale, the side garden porch is a stand-in for a country house entrance and made all the more so by the puny city stoop entry in the driveway.

In contrast to the front pavilion, the rear pavilion is visible from the driveway, red, raised above the concrete wall, shows no visible support, is slightly larger in volume, and has larger corrugations on its surface. (Fig. 12) The differences between the front pavilion (with all its collisions and compacted qualities) and the freer volume in the back are clear. However, one also notices their equivalent half windows on either side of the concrete wall that suggest a relationship and the possibility that they were once a single entity. (see Fig. 1) It is not clear if it was a case of slipping and sliding or cutting and dicing, but some action has clearly occurred.

Thematic relationships continue across the site. Sitting in the middle of the plot, the east-west bar of the house establishes an *A-B-A* arrangement in the north-south direction by creating an equivalence between the city (the driveway) and the country (the compressed side garden). (Fig. 13) If we consider the entrance hall/interior garden to be part of the larger garden scheme, then it would not be unreasonable to consider the house a petrified version of the garden. In such a case, the garden is an expansive double width of the city and the driveway is just an access road to a garden site. (see Fig. 13)

Fig. 12

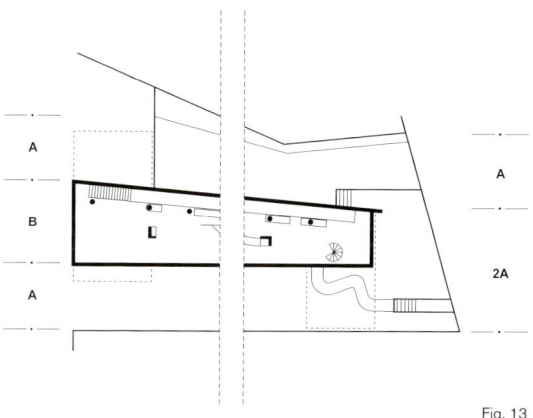

Fig. 13

SHOEHORNING THE SITE 37

A similar situation exists front to back (or east-to-west). The front yard is half the depth of the back yard. But if the entrance hall/interior garden is part of the larger garden scheme, then there is equivalence between the front and rear yards. (Fig. 14) Placing the house in the middle of the site could be seen as establishing the house as the initial object to be acted upon. Every action after the initial placement is in response to the context, program, or architect's intent. One of those actions is the alignment of the street pavilion with the south neighbor's house, while a following action is the shifting of the back (garden) pavilion beyond the north neighbor's house. (Fig. 15) The result reinforces the distinction between the urban front pavilion as compressed, contextual, and aligned, and the rear garden pavilion as free from such obligations.

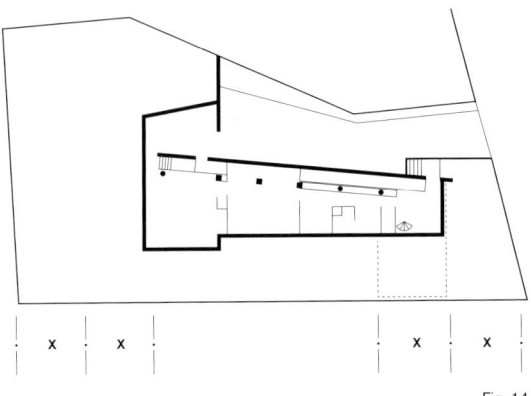

Fig. 14

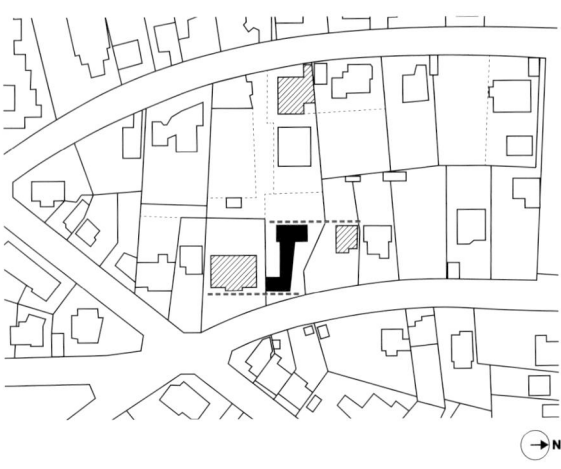

Fig. 15

Visitors enter from the street by passing through a gate, up some steps, down a meandering path, and through an artificial bamboo grove—or grand front porch—to the "front" door. This strategy reorients visitors that arrive from the street, a move made possible by the meandering path that connects the street to the front door. The "bamboo" porch is both a grove in the garden and a columned suburban front porch. The space that was once understood as a side garden adds to its identity by serving as a suburban front lawn as well.

Upon entering, visitors encounter a vestibule with a coatroom to one side and the interior garden/entrance hall to the other. The translucent screen that separates the two allows for the projection of shadows from the garden elements into the vestibule, slightly abstracting the encouter with nature. (see Fig. 10)

Koolhaas is relentless in compressing space. It seems that the bar of the main house is never thin enough; in the end, there is barely any habitable space. Behind the thick concrete wall, the ramp, stair, and storage wall with oversized columns compress the entry hall-dining room-kitchen-study-living room enfilade. The kitchen and its translucent wall are swung into the living space and leave only a corridor between the dining room and study. (Fig. 16) The cranking of the large concrete wall projects the kitchen into the space. The storage wall is the datum line and the glass garden wall is rendered even more ephemeral.

Fig. 16

On the second floor, the pool volume and walkway co-exist for the length of the bar. (Fig. 17) On the roof, there is so little space left that the pool deck overlaps the walkway below. It is only by turning the end bars 90 degrees and making them into pavilions that any reasonably proportioned space is made. Even then, the move seems to be made begrudgingly. The projection of the bar into the rear pavilion again forces a compression of the habitable space. (see Fig. 7)

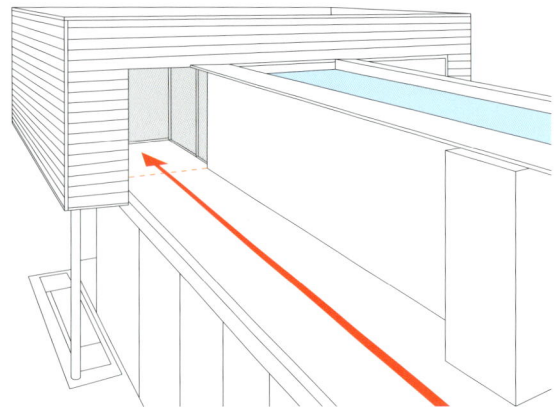

Fig. 17

The *A-B-A* arrangement of the house on the site is reiterated in the house organization. The *A-B-A* reappears in the general configuration of the house in a contemporary version as an *S* diagram of the house-bar and two pavilions. The *A-B-A* diagram also exists in the arrangement of the rooms. The kitchen serves as the center between the dining room and study, and the three of them together define a centered collection of spaces between the front hall and living room. (Fig. 18 & see Fig. 3) In addition, the *A-B-A* can also be seen in the bracketing of the living room by inside and outside stairs, and more generally, in the front hall by the steel stair and the ramp. The front pavilion upstairs could not operate more clearly in an *A-B-A* fashion. The rear pavilion is a little messier. (see Fig. 7) First, there is the equivalence between the external stair and the master bedroom closets. Second is the insertion of the bathroom-stair-hall combo in the middle and the similarly proportioned rooms, albeit one turned 90 degrees.

The *A-B-A* organization also exists in both section and elevation. On the north elevation, the concrete wall with voided center is clearly *A-B-A*, even if the center seems to be slipping into the garden. (Fig. 19) On the south elevation, the lower *A* gets buried (Fig. 20), but one knows that it is there by virtue of the skylight. (Fig. 21) Always one for balancing similarity and difference, Koolhaas differentiates the pavilion boxes by pushing one up and one down (see Fig. 18), transforming symmetry into a rotated *S* diagram.

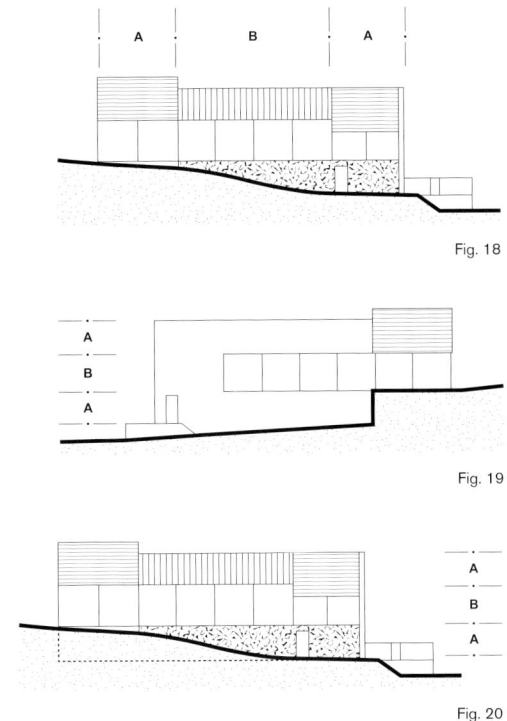

Fig. 18

Fig. 19

Fig. 20

In plan, Villa Dall'Ava as a whole is an *S* diagram, though it can also be understood as two *L*'s that connect the fronts and backs of each and that joins the city and country elevations. The garden pavilion is literally more separated from the house as it sits above the concrete wall. The sloping of the pool bottom links the elevated pavilion to the lower one by indicating the drop of the street pavilion into alignment with the top of the concrete wall. (see Fig. 11) This further differentiates the city pavilion from the garden pavilion and sets up the two as related yet different. Under the rear pavilion, the skylight in the basement library only allows for views of the trees, again reinforcing the difference between the compression that occurs at the street and the expansion that occurs in the garden.

The thematic differences between compression and expansion (i.e., city and garden) continue in the columns on the main floor. The front five are evenly spaced and collected in the storage wall; the last one is set free in the garden with boughs to hold up the red tree house. (see Fig. 3) A pairing of reversed promontories—one for the city and one for the garden—operate as two Casa Malapartes. The dining room, small and compressed, pushes into the double height entrance hall in the direction of the city; the living room sits level with the yard and projects into the expansive urban garden under the pavilion. (see Fig. 3) The plaster ceiling is the giveaway as the celestial pattern is separated in the middle. (Fig. 22)

Fig. 21

Fig. 22

Given Koolhaas's penchant for elaboration, it is not surprising that he defines elements and spaces in terms of one another: the red pavilion and the silver pavilion, the orange plastic fence and the chain link fence, the emphatic plane of the wall versus the volumes that sit adjacent to it, the fat and the thin columns, the plaster ceiling in the living room versus the corrugated ceiling above the front hall. But elements do not just exist in opposition to one another; they can also be iterated. The garden steps, stoop, ramp, circular stair, straight stair, a retractable ladder, and pool ladder represent iterations of vertical circulation. These exist as both elements and actions if one considers their formal attribues as being twisted, stacked, extended, or unwound and straightened out.

Elaboration does not end with the stairs; it can be seen again in the windows—specifically the strip windows. There are a total of seven windows in the house, more than enough to establish an inventory. First, there is the pure strip pavilion window facing the back garden. Second are the interrupted (and slipped) strip pavilion windows facing the drive and the street. On the backside of the front pavilion, the third window is an overscaled and cut strip that is made into a punched window. (see Figs. 5 & 6) On the rear pavilion, that same window becomes a fourth type, bent and pushed into the interior space of the house. (see Fig. 17) On the main floor, the floor-to-ceiling strip window wraps entirely around the space and is most identifiable by its near-absent quality. Finally, there is horizontal strip window to the basement. (see Fig. 21)

It would be an error not to mention the house's materiality. The present-yet-absent piano nobile has already been noted. On the main floor, Koolhaas deploys an array of systems for controlling light levels and views in and out: clear and etched glass, perforated and striated screens, lapped polyester and translucent walls. Not only is there a difference in material, but also in the relationship between the material and the glass: in front of, behind, part of, and removed from. Altogether, these conditions and arrangements replicate seasonal differences on a daily basis. Really, this is just stuff that is blowing in the wind between the ground and the habitable spaces floating above. (Fig. 23) The "ground" is relatively easy to claim and identify: the green terrazzo floor is just petrified grass. Where the house does emerge above the ground, the stone garden wall surrounds it.

The material theme for the elevated spaces above is much trickier to establish. Inside the house, the first-floor ceiling is a patterned plaster that mirrors the patterned surface on the ground. The corrugated metal on the underside of the rear garden box meets this plaster ceiling edge-to-edge. (Fig. 24) On the underside of the front pavilion, the continuity of the corrugated metal (from outside-to-inside) reinforces the idea of the continuity of the garden space.

But what is holding everything up? Even if one can fathom all of the present columns as supporting an open box beam pool on the roof, it would be difficult to believe that the front pavilion (with its openings spanning from the concrete wall to the too-thin porch columns) or the rear pavilion (supported by a single column with tiebacks) can do the work necessary to bear the weight of the pool. The trick is that it is all a single entity. Instead of being pavilions and containers or walls and impossibly thin columns, the end pavilions are part of a continuous dumbbell concrete structure. (Fig. 25) The corrugated metal is merely a curtain that conceals.

Fig. 23

Fig. 24

Fig. 25

On the roof, it is all ground: moss, water, and paving. (Fig. 26) Yet, the thinness of the ground cover here is just another curtain draped over the volume underneath. The water fills the volume to the brim. The two fencing types are completely happenstance and unpretentious, and recall the ephemerality of the curtains below, although the front orange construction fence does read something like a crown.

Villa Dall'Ava is a complex story that references the past while suggesting new possibilities for the future. Stuffed with references, deceptions, and creative embellishments, its materials are contemporary while its density of endeavor is a distinctly Parisian lineage that descends from houses like Maison de Verre and Villa Stein at Garches.

Fig. 26

SHOEHORNING THE SITE   45

Fig. 1

AS A CONSEQUENCE:
STIRLING'S NEUE STAATSGALERIE, STUTTGART

"'High' and 'low' are completely arbitrary and artificial distinctions that some bloated assholes invented to make life more complicated … The only thing that I care about in art is quality, intensity. Is a work of art capable of touching and moving me? Does it cause an emotional impact on me? Does it startle, surprise, upset, excite me? Does it make me think? Does it inspire me?"

- Gottfried Helnwein

There is no one better at subversion than Stirling. He subverts style, the monumental, and symmetry, all for the benefit of absorbing the context and accommodating the program. As a result, the Staatsgalerie is a modern mannerist masterpiece. There are endless references and organizational schemes, but all of them are slightly out of alignment. (Fig. 1)

Much of the Staatsgalerie's form is derived from frozen action. For all of the calm of the cornice aligning with the old museum, there is an enormous amount of slipping, sliding, bending, and breaking going on. Stirling's first move is to convert the galleries into a U-shape. It's easy to imagine that these new galleries were once a simple bar addition to the original building. In order to accommodate the elements on site, the bar has been pushed back and bent. (Fig. 2) The overscaled cornice on one face of the bar supports the frontal orientation of the bar while the indentation caused by the cylinder on the bar indicates the pushing action. (Fig. 3)

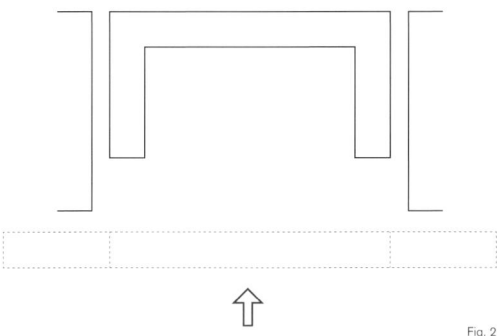

Fig. 2

Fig. 3

Colin Rowe argued that the Staatsgalerie has no elevation. In fact, it has two front elevations. The first is the wrapped courtyard elevation with an exaggerated cornice. The second elevation is more complex. The sheer ends of the galleries establish a surface, but few elements are in the same plane. The terrace attached to the theater is pulled out and holds the objects together with their stone material. Rowe is correct in that the trees somewhat blur this image, but there is little doubt that the combination of objects have an elevation-like presence on Konrad-Adenauer Strasse. (Fig. 4)

Fig. 4

Continuing the idea of the street elevation, it is interesting to note that Stirling brackets the new galleries with the existing building and the new theater building, but in a way that is out of alignment. (see Fig. 1) The theater apes the old museum by being made of stucco and stone; it is a blunt combination of stone below and stucco above. (Fig. 5) The old museum is a classical mix of the two materials. The theater has been pushed back to allow the old museum to hold the corner and act as the anchor of the extended complex. (Fig. 6)

The theater has also been bent to place its interior end on the side street. (Fig. 7) The resulting form of the theater puts the complex in scale with the adjacent apartment buildings. In case one were to miss the point, Stirling populates the recessed facade with domestically scaled windows. (see Fig. 5)

The south elevation of the theater supports its spurious location. The driveway retaining wall has pushed the stair off of the arched opening and extended the arch, causing all of the elements to pile up on one another. (Fig. 8) In addition to providing a second-floor projection for the lobby of the theater, the square window staples the upper and lower building together and reiterates the dynamic section of the hill. (Fig. 9)

Fig. 5

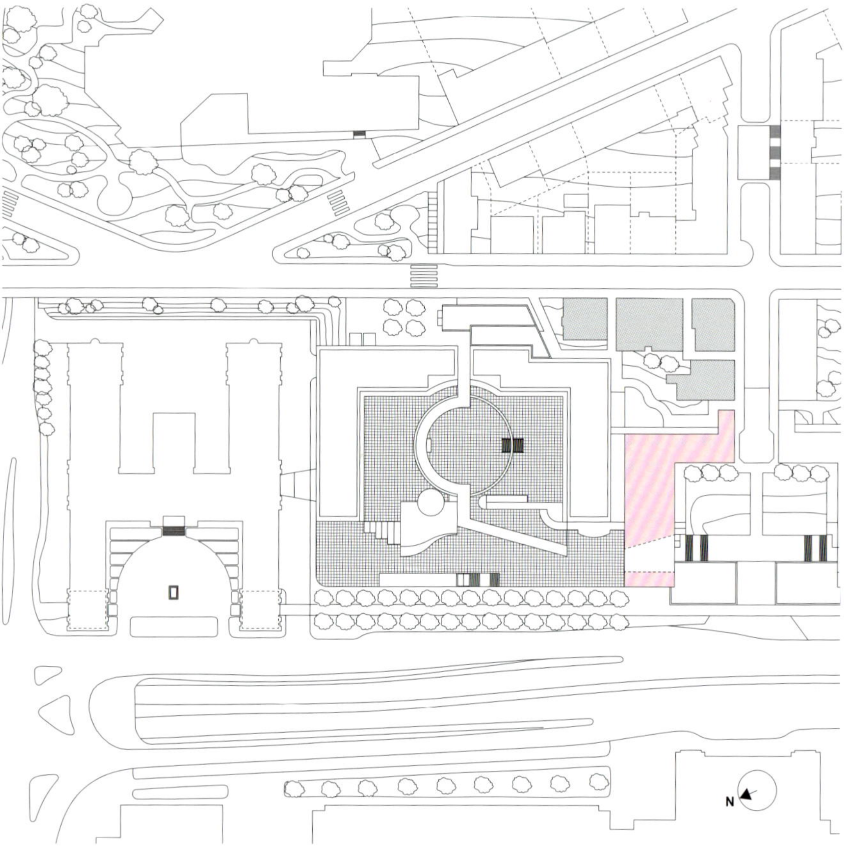

Fig. 6

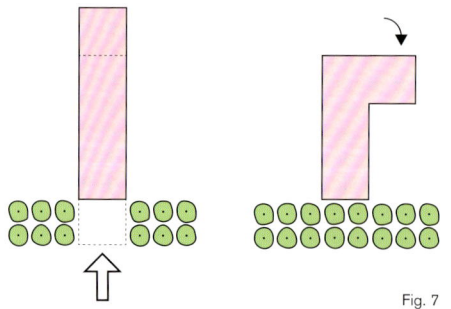

Fig. 7

Fig. 8

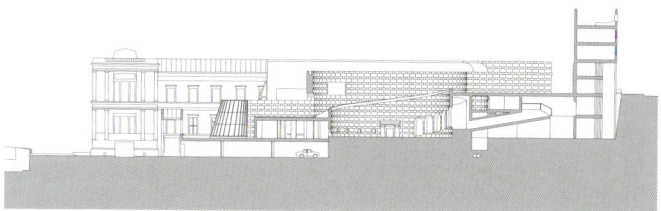

Fig. 9

There is another possible understanding of the theater building. One could imagine that to accommodate the south courtyard, the building had to be pushed to the north. (Fig. 10) Such an idea would go a long way in explaining the smaller galleries that are centered on the "U" and all of the squished elements on the terrace. (Fig. 11) There is little question that Stirling felt obliged to maintain the monumental scale of Konrad-Adenauer Strasse, even if only by fully lining it. The compression of the objects on the terrace makes them a more emphatic and contemporary version of the pavilions on the original museum. (Fig. 12)

A north-south compression also occurs in the temporary gallery, as indicated by the short span of the double row of columns, and in the auditorium, with the four closely grouped columns. (see Fig. 10) Acting as a gear, the bookstore has allowed the entrance pavilion to be rolled off axis. At the gallery level, the angled wall of the office building suggests that part of the building has been shifted to block the pedestrian path. Consequently, the glass wall of the administration building is crumpled. (Fig. 13).

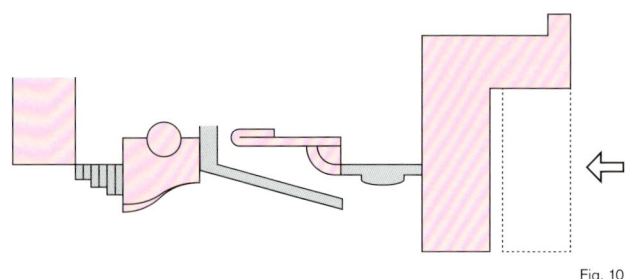

Fig. 10

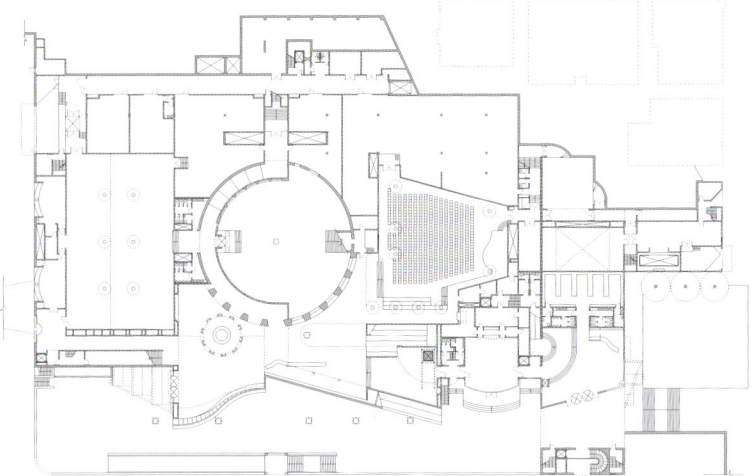

Fig. 11

Fig. 12

52 ARCHITECTURE STUFF

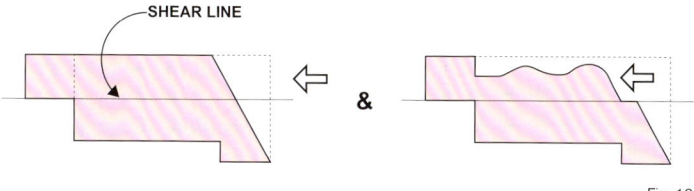

Fig. 13

Throughout the Staatsgalerie Stirling is obsessed with elaboration. There is never just one of anything; paired elements express degrees of difference. The auditorium and temporary gallery are good examples: they bracket the court, are lowered, and have stepped ceilings and flared columns. However, the columns are distributed differently in each, with one space containing seating and the other containing partitions. (Figs. 14 & 15)

Fig. 14

Fig. 15

The scuppers at the ends of the gallery wings are even more elaborated. In isolation, their off-center locations seem odd. They have either slipped sideways in deference to the center court or the wings have been compressed to bring them together. They make more sense when seen in combination with other elements. On the north wing, the scuppers and Florentine window make a centered composition on the facade. (Fig. 16) On the south wing, the scuppers are pulled off-center to align with the cafe below. (Fig. 17)

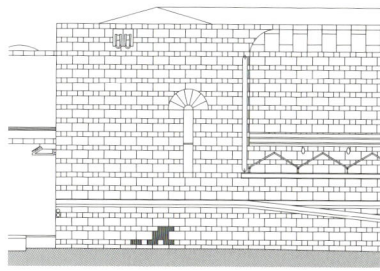

Fig. 16

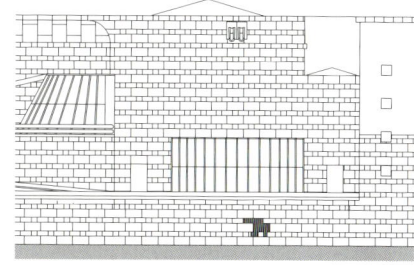

Fig. 17

AS A CONSEQUENCE   53

Another example of elaboration is the collection of entrance doors to the sculpture court from the north and south gallery wings. Typically, they would align. Here, the addition of the gallery ramp shortens the elevation on the south wing. (Fig. 18) These are two different configurations that result in different symmetrical door arrangements and an off-center gallery door in the northeast corner.

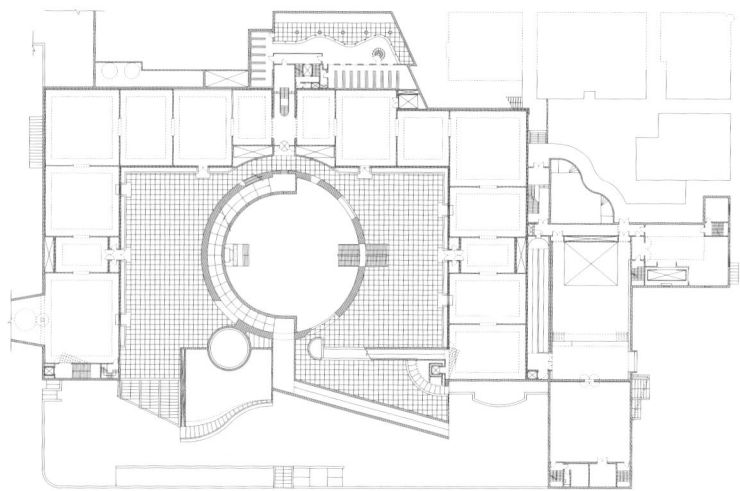

Fig. 18

If one understands the bracketing of the new galleries by both the old museum and the theater as a kind of enclosure, then one finds it at least two more times: with the new gallery wings and with the double wall of the circular courtyard. In addition, the U-shaped courtyards in front of the old museum and the side street to the south bracket the ensemble in between. (Fig. 19) The circular court establishes its presence as an object in juxtaposition to the wings that bracket it. However, on the entry level it remains in competition with and is bracketed by the temporary gallery and the auditorium. (Fig. 20) There are more bracketed conditions: the stair and ramp that bracket the baldachin entrance pavilion, the bracketing of the stair and ticket booth on the way to coat storage at the front of the theater, the lobbies that bracket the cafe, and the bracketing of the glass canopies to the galleries and the theater. The ramp to the galleries is bracketed by the same number of stairs up and down. (see Fig. 11) Although there are the occasional symmetries in the Staatsgalerie, Stirling is much more interested in equivalences such as stair-to-ramp or temporary gallery-to-auditorium. The pairing and bracketing allow him to show differences and similarities at the same time.

54 ARCHITECTURE STUFF

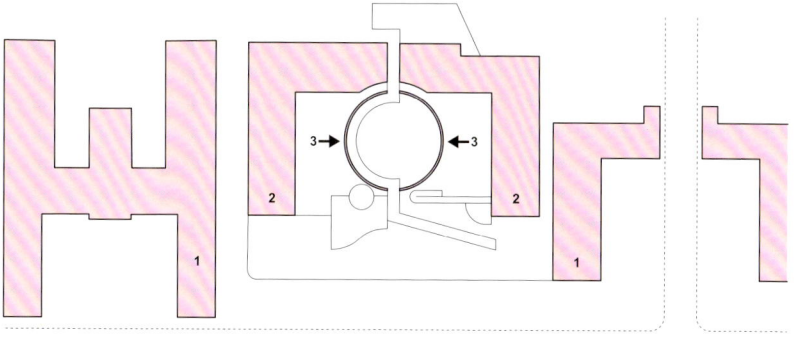

Fig. 19

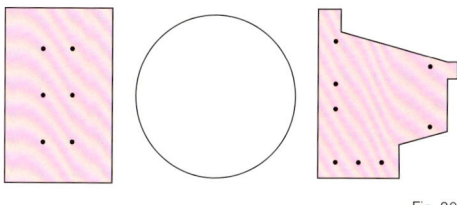

Fig. 20

The bracketing also allows for a strategy of *fleeting centers*. On the ground level, the center of the old museum is both emphatic and denied: it can only be approached by the circular drive. The new center of the complex is the steel baldachin, but this axis is immediately denied, and one is forced to move up the ramp to the left or the stair to the right. (Fig. 21) The same is true for the street entrance to the theater, where the choice is between an elevator on one side and a semicircular stair on the other. On the terrace, all of the elements are pavilions that front the plaza, but access is always shunted to the side.

The main museum entrance is around a corner, the pedestrian path through the site is on a diagonal, the cafe is frontal, but its entrance is in a recess to the side, and the theater entrance is out of sight, under the building, and on the diagonal with its glass canopy pulled to the side and facing the adjacent square. At the sculpture terrace level, the circular court has to be the center. But with the path to one side, the viewing windows all around, and the change in section (Fig. 22), it is more like the cross contours in the garden at Vaux-le-Vicomte.

Fig. 21

Fig. 22

The pedestrian path through the site is a good example of fleeting centers and the conflict between center and edge. Starting at the baldachin, there is the immediate move up the ramp that edges the terrace. One reverses direction across the terrace and is centered on the theater passthrough. Reversing again, one is centered on the diagonal ramp that leads to the edge of the front court. Turning right, one is centered on the rotunda. Upon entering the rotunda, one is required to move along its edge to the left and around. At the far side of the rotunda, one is again on-axis and must move through a tunnel until confronted with the wall of the administration building that blocks the path and forces a turn along the upper face of the museum, A final turn centers one on the crosswalk. (Fig. 23) The sequences to the galleries and theater have equally complex processions, albeit at 90 degrees to one another. In each case, the distinctions between center and edge are difficult to make out. (Fig. 24)

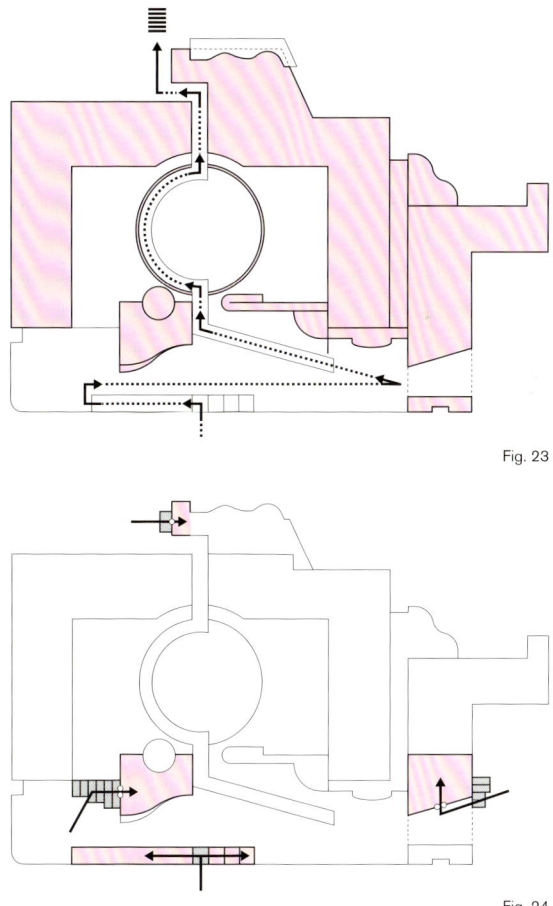

Fig. 23

Fig. 24

Glass canopies represent yet another elaboration of elements and occur as gabled ends or folded plates that establish a hierarchy of entrances to the building's programmatic entities. The baldachin and the entry to the administration building are each a single bay. (see Fig. 21) The entrance to the museum is three bays while the entrance to the theater is two bays. (Fig. 25 & see Fig. 8) A further distinction is made by their respective lengths. The baldachin is six glass panels deep, the administration canopy is three panels deep, the theater canopy is both three and six panels deep, and the museum is six, nine, and twelve panels deep. The baldachin and museum entrances are oriented east-and-west, entered frontally, and exited laterally. The administration and theater entrances are oriented north-and-south. The administration canopy is entered and exited frontally. The theater canopy is both dead-ended and exited on the diagonal. The entrance canopy to the site stands alone while the others are hung off the building on overscaled hangers. This bit of structural expressionism is not only a sop to his English friends Foster and Rogers, but also completes the history of architecture to the then-present. The various entrances incorporate cylindrical red revolving doors in relationship to the canopies: one for the administration and two each for the theater and museum. The museum doors are lateral to the canopy while the theater doors are removed from their canopy.

Fig. 25

The circulation systems, windows, and portals are also elaborated. (Fig. 26) For vertical circulation, there are ramps, stairs, and elevators, and they come in numerous forms. (Figs. 27, 28, 29, & 30) For the ramps, there is a meandering pedestrian ramp, an object ramp, and a ramp enclosed in a room. They vary in their sectional qualities and spatial enclosure. Stairs occur in straight, curved, and switchback forms; they are long or short, wide and narrow. The elevators are open and closed, object and void, visible and hidden.

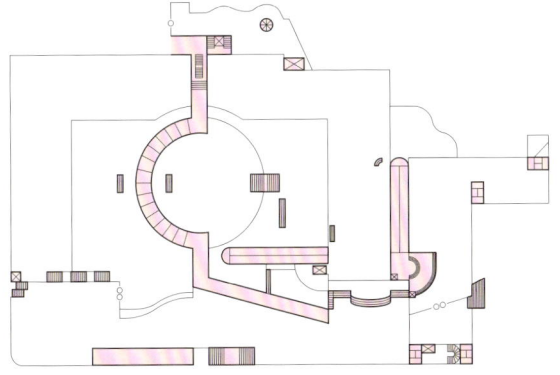

Fig. 26

Fig. 27

Fig. 28

Fig. 29

AS A CONSEQUENCE 59

Fig. 30

There are three types of windows and portals: historical, vernacular, and abstract. The abstract come in three forms: round, square, and all glass/void. The vernacular openings are punched, domestic in scale, and relate to the adjacent apartment houses. The many historical references cover the history of architecture. There is an Egyptian portal into the garage (see Fig. 21), an Etruscan entrance to the temporary gallery (Fig. 31), overscaled Romanesque windows and passages in the central sculpture court (Fig. 32), a Florentine Romanesque window by the museum entry (see Fig. 16), a rusticated portal in the theater service wing (Fig. 33), mannerist missing stones in the plinth (Fig. 34), modernist strip windows in the office building (Fig. 35), a deep strip window with a yellow column in the theater wing (see Fig. 8), the large glass wall of the library (see Fig. 35), the curving and sloped glass wall of the entrance pavilion (Fig. 36), the pediment transitions between galleries (Fig. 37), and the gridded glass gallery entrances. (Fig. 38)

Each of the windows and portals has work to do. The representational quality of the Florentine Romanesque window transforms it into a piece of art hung next to the entry. It is large in scale due to its honorific place. Equally, the strip windows in the office block announce the museum to the neighborhood and the working aspect of the museum. The three-story glass wall of the library wraps the diagonal wall back into the site, indicating that there was more facade than would fit on the street; it is a subtle way to invite people through a hidden pedestrian path.

Fig. 31   Fig. 32

Fig. 33   Fig. 34   Fig. 35

Fig. 36   Fig. 37   Fig. 38

If the driveway wall in the south court pushed the arched opening into the horizontal slot window, it also reinforces the idea that facades are slippery things. It is just as easy to imagine that the theater entrance was once attached to its canopy but slid onto axis with the portal facing Konrad-Adenauer Strasse and pulled the slot window with it. (Fig. 39 & see Fig. 8).

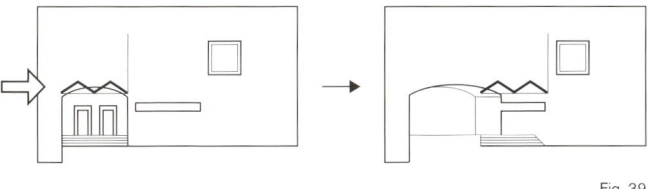

Fig. 39

The void in the plinth caused by the stones falling on the ground is pure folly and a quote from any English Romantic garden. Stirling was proud of the quality of construction that he got at the Staatsgalerie and only in this instance could he entertain decay before its time. It is interesting to note that the Staatsgalerie was under construction at the same time that Cambridge was threatening to tear down the History Faculty Library because the tiles were falling off. The irony of Stirling's historical quotes is further indicated by the placement of the historicist columns and entablature at the entrance to the temporary gallery half underground. Either he is excavating them or indicating that literal historicism is about to be buried. (see Fig. 31)

The abstract openings that are square, round, or voided are no less engaged; they are literally scattered about. The round window in the stucco above the theater arch on the entry terrace has simply rolled along the stone wall into place. (Fig. 40) The two round windows circled in stone on the ramp to the galleries are equally at loose ends. (Fig. 41) The stacked round windows in the administrative block (Fig. 42) on the main axis are crossovers between the abstract and the historical; they could easily be from any number of 1930s international style buildings. The stacked square windows on the end elevation of the theater work in the same manner, though they recall a more fascist 1930s architecture. In addition, they look like sprocket holes that allowed the stucco of the building to be rolled up from the stone facade or the stone facade to have been rolled down to reveal the stucco. (see Fig. 5) The same is true of the windows on the north and south elevations of the theater; they look like sprocket holes that allowed the building to move back and forth in an east-west direction. (see Figs. 8 & 40)

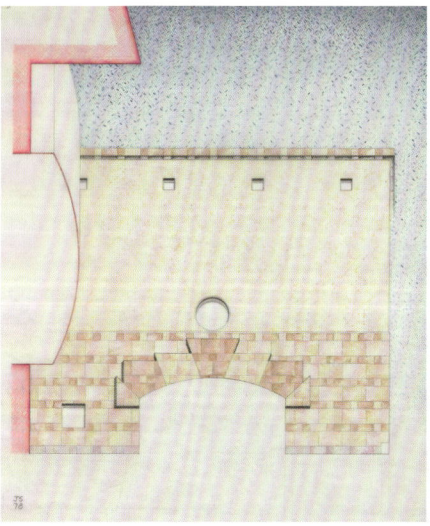

Fig. 40

Fig. 41

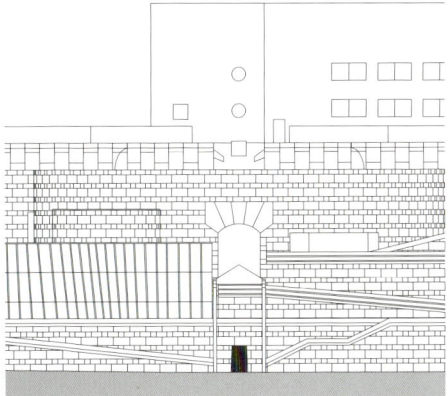

Fig. 42

The overscaled pipe handrails can't be missed. At the terrace entry level, the railing is a single pipe high. At the gallery level, the railing is two pipes high. One might presume that the difference is to allow the railings to act as mock entablatures and to keep them in scale with their respective facades. (Fig. 43) The difference also allows one to understand that the pedestrian path is dropped from the upper level. The bright red and blue of the railings are shocking and ribbon-like against the weight and neutrality of the stone. As such, they demonumentalize the building and pretend to be a wayfinding device. The curvy walls of the library and entrance pavilion are more abstracted ribbon ends that—once again—bracket the ensemble.

Fig. 43

The bright color of the handrails is an introduction to the use of color in the project. In general, color is used to lighten the mood. Specifically, the colored elements reinforce the idea that for all the historical references, this is a contemporary building. The green of the lobby floor and the green window mullions place the lobby outside of the museum. (Fig. 44) The entry ensembles, the yellow mushroom column that pierces the slot window while holding up the arch, and the straphangers holding up the canopies are brightly painted elements that advertise their incongruity. The mechanical system that is essential for a museum is invisible except for the grossly overscaled blue and green ventilators on the administration plaza. (Fig. 45)

Fig. 44

Fig. 45

A certain subversion occurs with respect to the monumental aspects of the building as well. The bracketing allows for what is seemingly monumental. Upon closer inspection, it all breaks down and goes awry. Movement from center to edge seems to have a peculiar relationship with a pinball machine by transforming what were once formal processions into constantly redirected and emergent routes. The result is an idea of style that is expanded: the monumental is undercut and axial directionality is redefined.

From day one, Stirling was the bad boy of architecture. At the Staatsgalerie, he enhanced this reputation by subverting style, mixing the monumental with play, and absorbing the context. Even the materiality of the Staatsgalerie is a stick in the eye: no self-respecting modernist would build in stone and no self-respecting classicist would expose the steel or be so playful with the stone and glass.

Fig. 1

PILING IT ON:
VANNA VENTURI HOUSE

"As we have already seen in the case of 'bricolage' ... there are several solutions to the same problem. The choice of one solution involves a modification of the result to which another solution would have led, and the observer is in effect presented with the general picture of these permutations at the same time as the particular solution offered."

- Claude Lévi-Strauss

Big and little, modest and grand, unified and discrete, abstract and circumstantial, the Vanna Venturi House provides ample references to the whole history of architecture. (Fig. 1) More specifically, this house is a further development of the modernist idea of spatial extension as seen in such projects as the Barcelona Pavilion, where the space flows from inside to out (or the reverse) through an expansive roof, extended walls, and glass planes. Venturi has much more to say about spatial extension than that. Here he adds to the somewhat singular modernist repertoire by extending space through changes in scale, slipping and sliding, compression, overlap, transparency, bending, and layering. (Fig. 2)

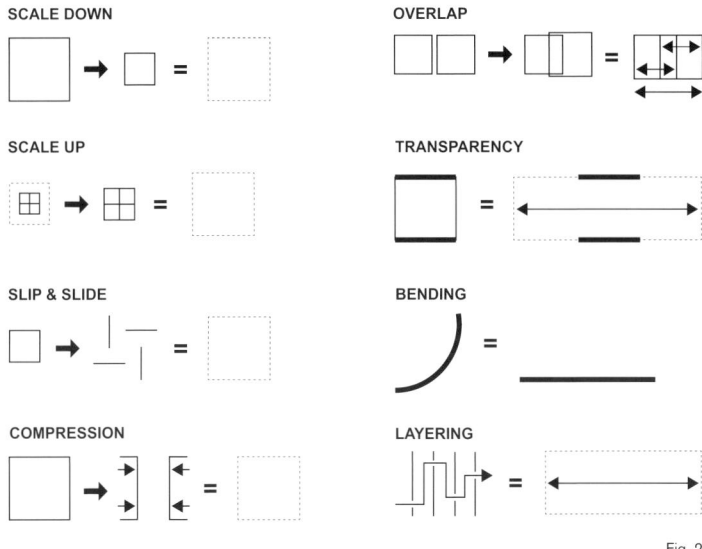

Fig. 2

Situated on a suburban street where the houses are typically much closer to the road, the Vanna Venturi House announces itself from its own back yard. (Fig. 3) Perhaps a bit squat, it recalls the McKim Mead and White Low House, though it would be easy to imagine that it is sitting in a valley and only the top half is visible. Considering the double dado, it would be easy to believe that the house has been compressed with one story overlaid on another. (Fig. 4) The cant of the driveway leaves little doubt that Venturi is referencing the cranked axis from the Propolea to the Parthenon. (Figs. 5)

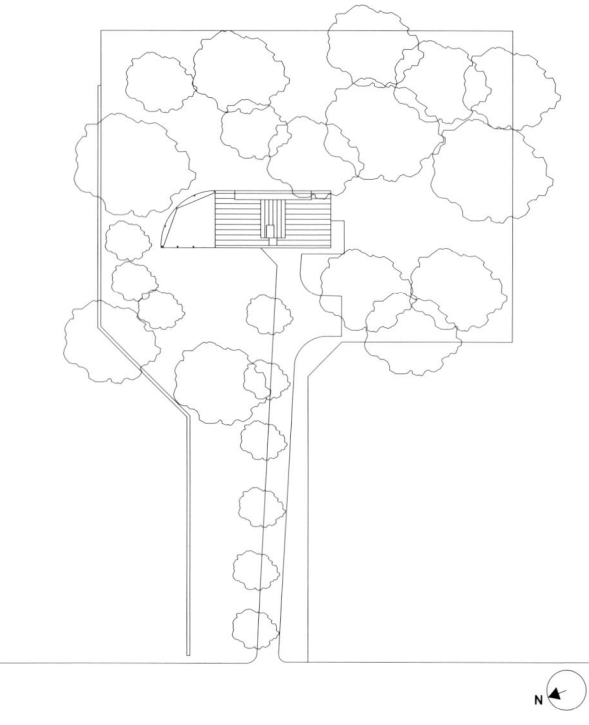

Fig. 3

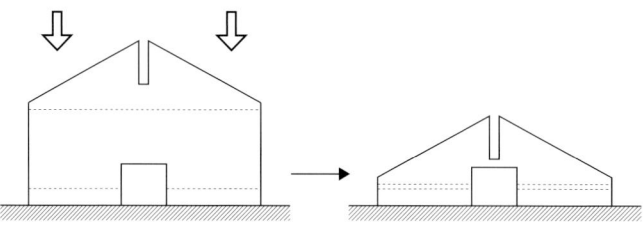

Fig. 4

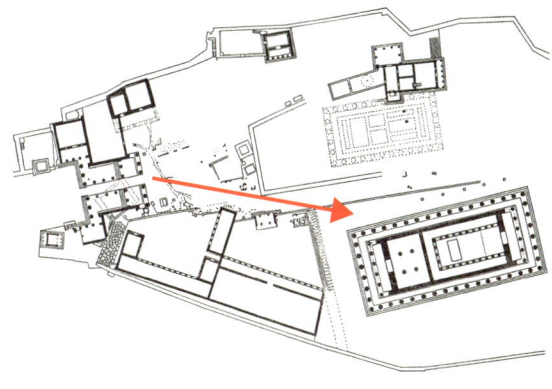

Fig. 5

The front elevation is loaded with movement. Most obvious is the split pediment or dueling shed roofs, a historical reference to Moretti's Casa Il Girasole. (Fig. 6). Clearly the intent is to pack a lot into a little. There is also the compression expressed in the compacted (and once square) entry, the segmented arch, and the double dado. The segmented arch cannot actually be supporting anything; it exists as a graphic device that references the thermal window on the rear facade while tying the lone small bathroom window on one side of the entry with the five that are opposite. Looking at the blank wall next to the strip window, it could be argued that the small bathroom window has been loaned to the four-square window on one side to balance the two sides.

Fig. 6

The strip window is oddly proportioned and oddly placed for a conventional suburban house, but it remains contained and punched. There is no dado between it and the end wall, appearing cast to the edge of the building and pulled in by the two string courses. However, it is the lally column behind and centered on the middle window that is most troubling. (see Fig. 1) This little column is a small indication of the fact that there is no limit to the elements that can be quoted. In case this reference to modernist piloti is too subtle, an unframed void window with a pencil-line sill (representing abstract modernist ideals) lurks in the shadow of the entry porch behind the front facade. (Fig. 7)

Fig. 7

Clearly, the chimney is an essential element of the facade. It is simultaneously big, little, chimney, wall, and object. As an object, it is essential as a backdrop to the cartoon house facade in front and a masterful reversal of the typical object-wall relationship. The fact that the big chimney and house facade are centered on one another emphasizes the house's monumental character. The fact that the small chimney is the same width of the slot and off center makes it clear that something has shifted. This is a theme that is reiterated endlessly in the house.

In the entry porch alone, one is reminded of horizontal compression several times, first in the overextended lintel. No lintel would need that much bearing. (see Fig. 1)

The width of the porch opening must have been compressed, though it is possible that the lintel is a track on which the shed facades move back and forth. There is also a second-floor bathroom that is shifted into the porch space, pushing the big plate glass window to the right and the entry doors below onto the sidewall. (Figs. 8 & 9) The small-scale space on the left and the taller space on the right help to shift the entry axis. (Fig. 10)

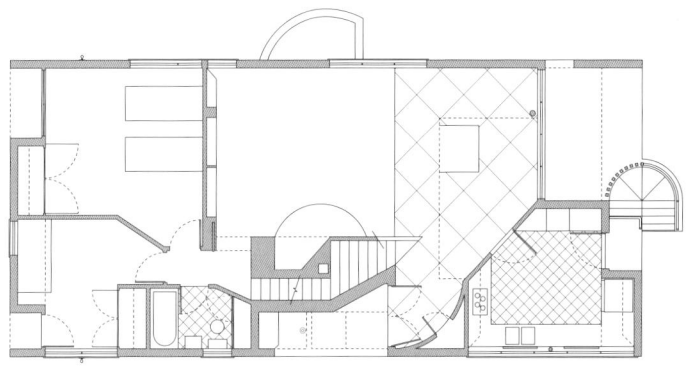

Fig. 8

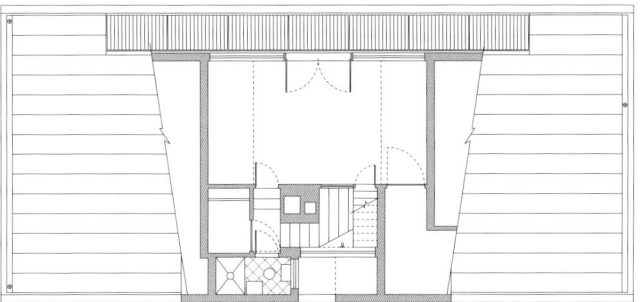

Fig. 9

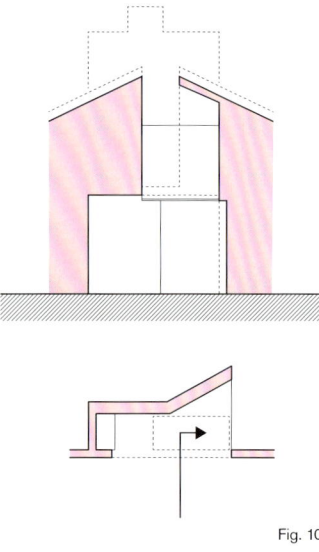

Fig. 10

The compression and shifting are no less adamant in the vertical dimension. On the rear wall of the porch, the big window functions as a castle entrance that has been lifted. This move allows visual access through the window, even if it is a little high and the actual entrance door is to the right, a procession borrowed from the Temple of Apollo at Didyma. The raising of the wall gives the chimney its height and provides a higher space and clerestory lights on the second floor. (Fig. 11) And yet, either the entrance void has not been lifted high enough or the big chimney has been compressed, leaving one lonely stack. In either case, the grand and the modest are allowed to co-exist.

Entering the front porch, there are two aspects that are immediately apparent: the space is shallow and the door has slipped to the wall on the right. Clearly there are two forces at work: back-to-front compression and slipping. In contrast to the grand facade, the entrance sequence indicates that this is a modest house. Only two entities remain grand: the double front door and the abstract voided window, each the same size as the other. Their equivalence and displacement hints at the fact that they once occupied the same place and that the compression of the entry has disconnected them. The size of the two elements allows for retaining a sense of grandeur while emphasizing modesty, as the double door needs to be pushed in under the porch wall to fit. (see Fig. 10) Passing through the front door, the theme of compression is continued in the tiny front hall and miniscule hall closet. The quarter circle in plan does its job by exaggerating the length of the wall and redirecting the axis from the front door to the rear garden wall. The curved wall can also be understood as the result of the kitchen having been pushed into the entry space. (Fig. 12)

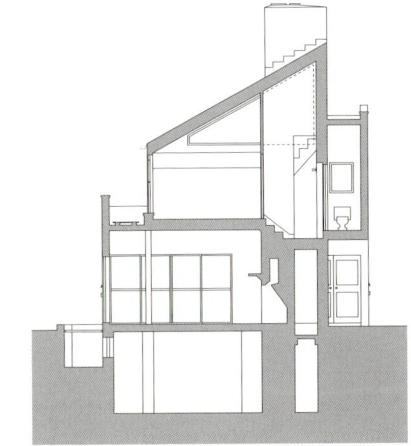

Fig. 11

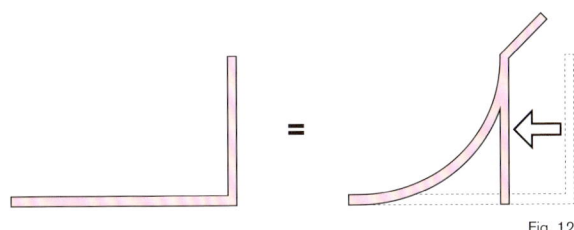

Fig. 12

As for extending space, expansion is made clear in the (designed but unbuilt) fenced yard. (see Fig. 3) The straight front wall is a modernist extension of space from the slot window of the small front bedroom (and in alignment with the whole of the monumental front facade). The curved back wall is the same as the foyer entry hall: a quarter circle arc that marks a change in axis. (Fig. 13) Further, the two quarter circles are the beginning and end of a sequence from entry to walled garden and the redirected axis is a direct reference to any number of houses by Edwin Lutyens.

The living and dining rooms build upon a theme of *too much stuff in too little space*. If one manages not to trip over the triangular stair that juts into the too-small hall, one would notice the over-scaled fireplace that has been jammed into the stair and appears to be the cause of the compression of the front porch. (Fig. 14 & see Fig. 8)

The wall between the porch and the stair seems like a large elastic band, and there is no assurance that the fireplace will not be propelled into the living room. (see Fig. 8) The angle of the kitchen wall in relation to the porch-stair-wall makes it easy to assume that the fireplace is actually frozen mid-launch. In a different action, the lateral direction

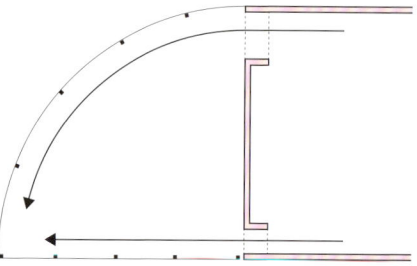

Fig. 13

Fig. 14

of the firebox (and its exaggerated taper on one side and straight edge on the other) suggests that it is moving toward the bedrooms. The off-centered hearth and flared chimney wall support this idea. (Fig. 15) As an additional way of exaggerating the scale of the space, the firebox is oversized and the mantle—trying to keep up—is too high and way too thin. (see Fig. 14)

An essential aspect of the living and dining rooms is their continuity versus discrete elements. The initial move is to mark the limits of the space with the pier in the living room bookshelves and the lally column in the dining room. However, including the dining terrace, the dining room becomes the center of an *A-B-A** sequence. If the bedroom is added to the consideration, the living room becomes the center of an *A-B-A** sequence of the main interior living spaces. (Fig. 16)

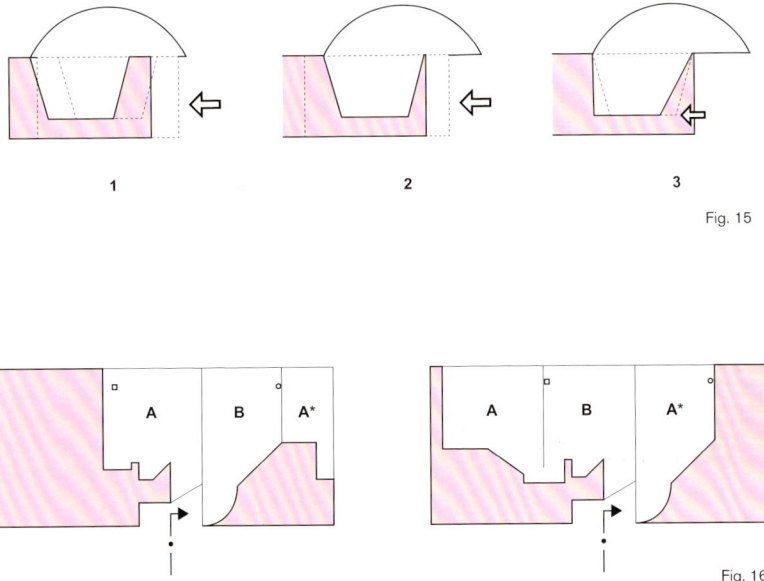

Fig. 15

Fig. 16

The critical discrete element is the arced ceiling in the dining room, which could have been caused by one of two forces: either the glass wall was pulled in from the far side of the porch or the once-solid wall was pulled up from the floor to reveal the glass wall. It is important to note that the edge of the resultant clerestory does not align with the change in floor material. The double height space allows the distinction between living and dining, but the overlap of the floor blurs the line between the two and allows for a continuity and extension of space. The three-panel window-door to the back garden emphasizes this fact by stapling the two conditions together. (Fig. 17)

It would also be fair to read everything in this sequence as shifted or sliding. The different lengths of the living room wall, the dining room wall, and the stair overlapping the dining room and hall support this idea. The vertical window in the living room and the vertical slot on the porch can also be read in this manner, as seemingly identical forms would be used comparably. Flattening the ceiling in the dining room would extend it to include the dining porch slot. (Fig. 18) The living room slot window could have been formed by the bookcase wall sliding into the bedroom. (Fig. 19)

Fig. 17

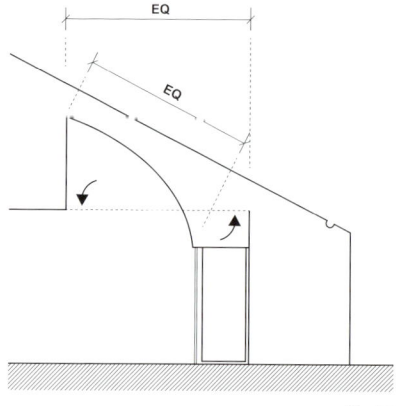

Fig. 18

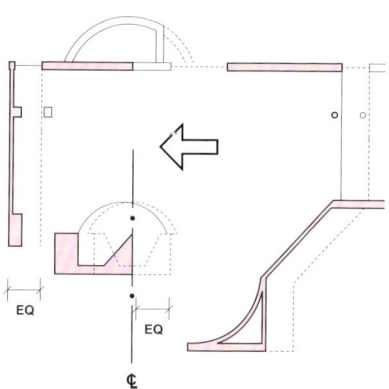

Fig. 19

Fig. 20

The shifting and compression in the house do not just happen in the lateral direction, they also occur front-to-back. In the living room the compression of the fireplace has already been discussed, but there is also a misalignment of the shelving supports and the segmented arched headers in the living room bookcase. (Fig. 20) It is hard to tell if the arches are caused by a slight compression or—as the two vertical supports for the shelf would suggest—an expansion when the second floor was pushed down on the first. The two bare bulbs in the ceiling that are centered on the decorative arches reinforce their primacy. If that is true, then both the pier and the vertical support for the shelves have been pushed into the space. (Fig. 21) There are other elements that suggest that both the living and dining spaces (and, in fact, the whole house) should be much larger and are only temporarily compressed. In the dining room, the slippage of the arced ceiling past the glass porch wall would make it appear as if the rear garden wall has been pushed into the house and is further supported by the compression that occurs on the exterior side kitchen wall. (Fig. 22) The scale of the floor tiles in the dining area and the scale of the fireplace both support the idea that only a fragment of the living and dining rooms are present.

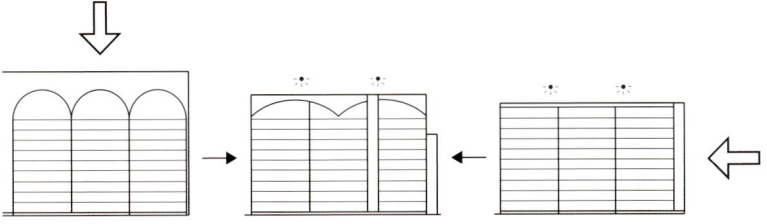

Fig. 21

PILING IT ON 77

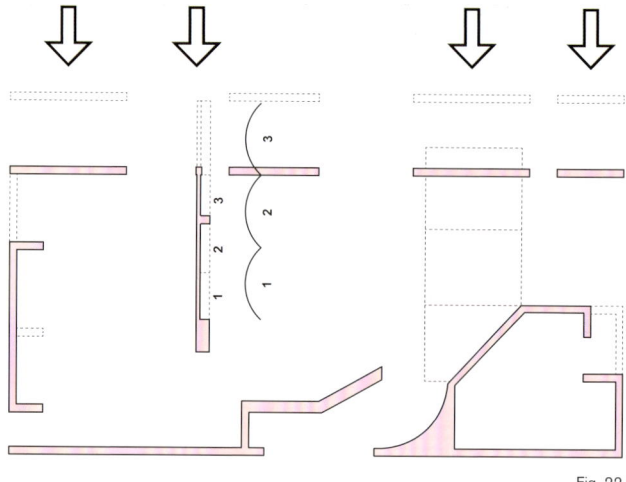

Fig. 22

In the vertical dimension, the compression that was registered on the front and back elevations remains evident where the first-floor spaces are pushed up into the roof zone. In the living room and dining room, the shift is obvious in the lowered soffit of the dining terrace and in the small hall that leads to the basement stair and bedrooms. However, it is in the upstairs bedroom that the compression of the roof or the extension of the ground-floor volume is most clear. (Fig. 23)

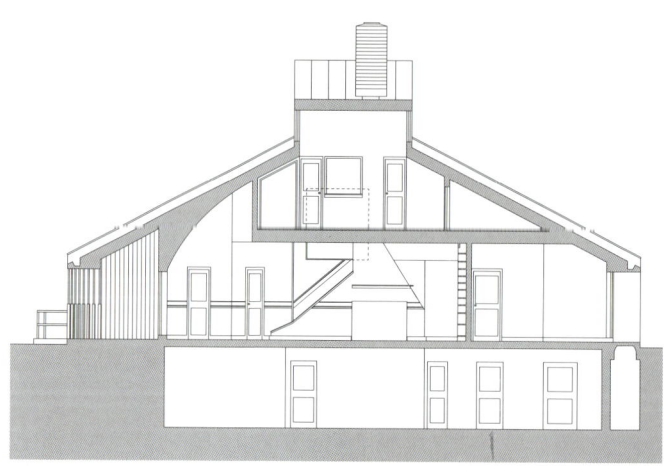

Fig. 23

Traveling to the second floor via the open and severely compressed (2'-4") stair makes the double allusion obvious. (Fig. 24) First, the chimney has been turned into a buttress for the front wall, a clear aping of gothic cathedrals. Second, there is a distinction being made between the categories of served and service space. In general, the service spaces appear to be collected behind the front facade. Neither space is pure, as one is allowed to bleed into and borrow from the other. The fireplace is clearly in the service zone. But by being offset as an object, the fireplace appears to sit in the living room, thus adding five feet to the 15-foot depth of the room. The reverse is true of the outside cellar stair. In addition to Venturi's humor of pushing the heroic modernist object (the bull nose stair) into the ground, the service stair extends into the served space. (see Fig. 8 & Fig. 25)

Fig. 24

Fig. 25

On the end elevations, Venturi equates solid with service space and void with served space. The side kitchen wall is most clear about this relationship, as it is scraped back to reveal the utilities for the house yet remains solid. (see Fig. 25) On the bedroom side, two things happen. First, the side wall of the small service component of the bedroom (closet and desk area) is removed from the front facade and pulls the connecting bedroom wall with it and into alignment with the kitchen wall, marking the extent of the service zone on opposing sides of the house. (Fig. 26) Second, the so-called service solid of the bedroom is punched with a window to announce its accommodation of the served. (Fig. 27)

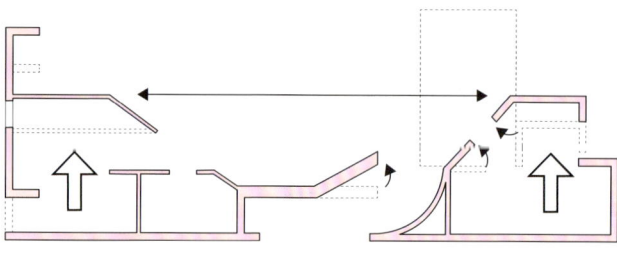

Fig. 26

The second floor is all artist garret: nothing but light, air, and architectural conceits. Clearly this space has no business being 10 feet off the ground. The stair-to-nowhere confirms the fact that this was once an attic that has been compressed on to a second floor. (Fig. 28) In the lateral direction, the shed roofs have been pulled in, allowing

Fig. 27

only a 10-foot-wide central space. The balcony marks the extent of the compression. (Figs. 29 & 30) On the front, the bathroom has been pushed into the porch volume. Front-to-back, the compression is so strong that the closet has been pushed out of the room and is now found on the stair landing. (see Fig. 9) Light is provided by the thermal window and clerestory windows. Air is easily available on the balcony. It is the quotes made by the thermal window (borrowing from Rome, Palladio, Penn Station, and Kahn) and the stair-to-nowhere (Fig. 31) that further express the fact that this house was designed for an architect's self-amusement.

Fig. 28

PILING IT ON   81

Fig. 29

Fig. 30

Fig. 31

Moving outside again, the symmetry of the shed roofs, thermal window, railing slot, and sloped ends of the wall make clear the slippage of the ground-floor openings and the small chimney. Taken as a set, the rear garden windows appear to be entrances to three completely separate entities that are located by convenience on this elevation. (see Fig. 27) If this is another architectural quote, the shop fronts on Bramante's House of Raphael are a clear candidate. (Fig. 32) A second indication of this slippage is the ship's light atop the blank wall on the rear elevation. Straight through the house on the front, a similar light is centered above the foursquare window (Fig. 33), and another marks the center of the north elevation around the corner. (see Fig. 27)

Fig. 32

PILING IT ON   **83**

On the rear garden elevation, the thermal window is removed from the facade, as was the modernist void window in the front. This is Rowe and Slutzky's phenomenal transparency at its best: a layering that establishes an edge or threshold and allows it to be broken in order to create an extension of space. The gable is never allowed to be complete on either the garden facade or the thermal window facade. Instead—on the oblique—the shed roof in the back is presented as both the open lid of an overstuffed box and as the support for the front facade.

Finally, given the abstraction and neutral quality of all the house materials, the exposed brick of the chimney is a surprise. Like the revealed utilities at the kitchen door, the compression across the whole has exposed the innards. Given all the references to architectural history, the chimney presents itself as a piece of a folly ruin sitting on top. (Fig. 34)

In the end, we are forced to return to the essential identities of the house as big and little, modest and grand, unified and discrete, abstract and circumstantial; it is a lesson in the history of architecture that is both compressed and extended.

Fig. 33

Fig. 34

Fig. 1

PRIMORDIAL PRESENCE:
KAHN'S KIMBELL ART MUSEUM

"The historical sense involves a perception, not only of the pastness of the past, but of its presence."

- T.S. Elliot

This is Kahn at his best: basic volumes transformed, simple yet innovative structure, nuanced light sources, endless elaboration, and flexible modulation. The Kimbell Art Museum is best known for the vaults that recall their Roman predecessors and the train cars that Kahn once rode from Philadelphia to New Haven. It is both a compressed Roman bath and a rail yard. (Fig. 1) The vaults are capable of containing everything: porticos, galleries, library, cafe, auditorium, conservation studio, bookstore. Together, the vaults make a modulated loft space that is neither a warehouse nor a traditional gallery. (Fig. 2)

Fig. 2

Served space and service space is a well-known theme in Kahn's work. Here the low spaces between the galleries are both service space and not. As service space, they are ancillary to the vaulted galleries and provide a domestic scale for the viewing of small paintings and objects. They are even more service-like when the panels are pulled perpendicular into the vaults, enabling the low spaces to seemingly operate as storage bins from which the panels have been pulled into the lit vaulted galleries. (Fig. 3) As served spaces, they are the planar ceiling of the gallery and provide for a continuity of the whole while the vaults act as skylights.

The service aspect of the low spaces is reinforced by containing the ducts, fire stairs, and storage rooms. (Figs. 4 & 5) They also contain the bifurcated processional stair from the lower lobby. (Fig. 6) It is clear that service and served spaces are not as rigorously defined as one might expect; each can borrow from the other. The literal edge between the low spaces and the vaults is blurred. On the floor, the travertine of the low spaces extends into the vaulted spaces while the vault seemingly compresses the flat aluminum ceiling panels of the low spaces. (see Fig. 3)

Fig. 3

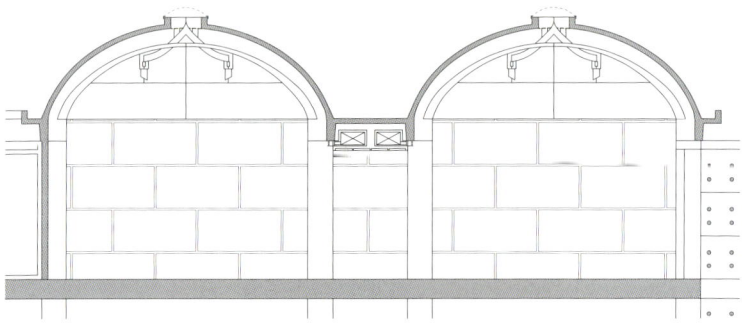

Fig. 4

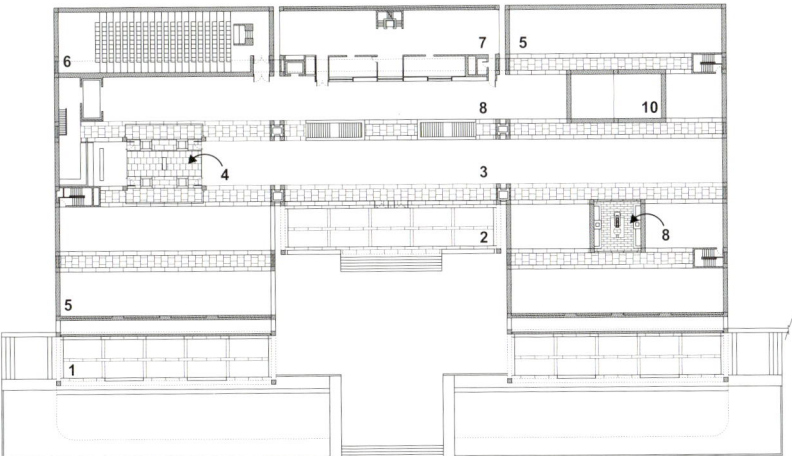

1. LOGGIA 2. PORCH 3. ENTRANCE 4. GREEN COURT 5. GALLERY 6. AUDITORIUM 7. LIBRARY
8. BOOKSTORE 9. WATER COURT 10. CONSERVATOR BELOW

Fig. 5

Fig. 6

If the modulation between the vaults and low spaces were not enough, Kahn peppers the galleries with exterior spaces in order to further shape them. At the gallery level, they are legible as two double-square courtyards and two square courtyards. On the roof they read as four squares. The biggest courtyard is an insertion of the park into the west elevation, creating a recessed center with two wings. This is Fort Worth and not Versailles, but the sequence from the city to the park is remarkably similar from the hard forecourt to the garden. (Fig. 7) The tripartite organization is relentless in both cases and the chateau's enfilade rooms have now become the Kimbell's linear galleries. Nothing with Kahn is a straight crib, so it is not surprising to find the indented city facade of Versailles facing the park in the case of Fort Worth. (Fig. 8) In the case of the other courtyards, Kahn may be referring to the courtyards of Versailles but now leans more toward asymmetry and variation. Such deviations are always to make a point. In the case of the indented facade, Kahn wants better integration with nature and to de-monumentalize the museum with the placement of a recessed center. By elaborating the differences in the courtyards, he is able to make the classical contemporary, replacing symmetry with balance.

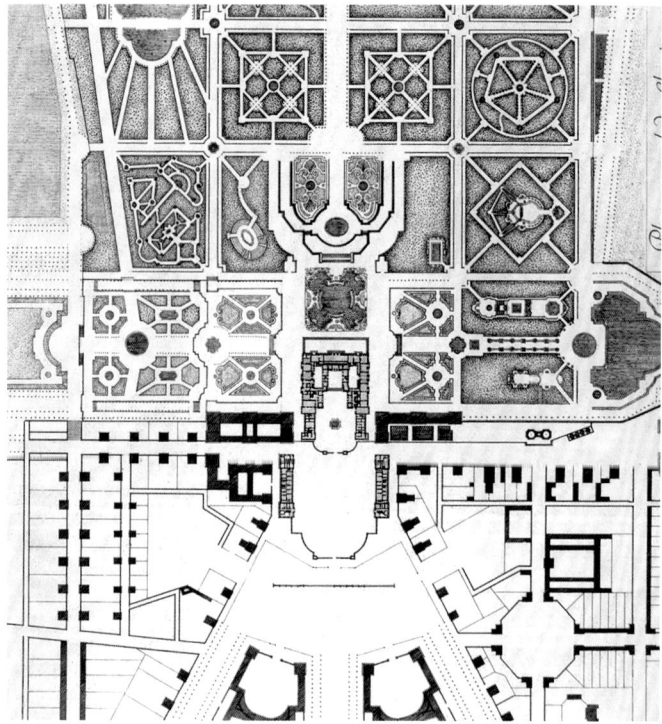

Fig. 7

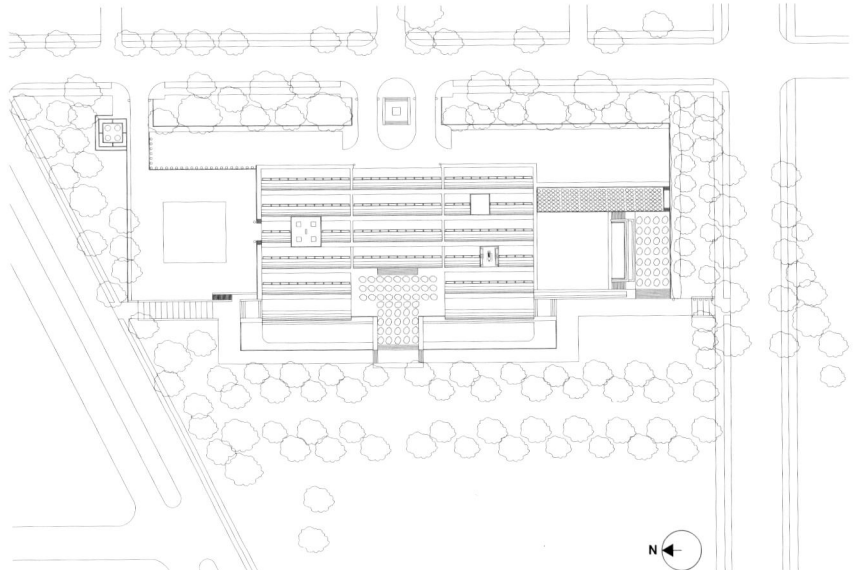

Fig. 8

The park court has one glass wall protected by the dislocated portico that now serves as a porch. More importantly, the court is filled with small trees that bring nature down to the scale of the art. The smallest courtyard—the water court—is a simple square in the south wing where the vault has been removed. It has two glass walls that run along the edge of the vault and face the low areas and two solid walls that accentuate the interruption of the vault. On center with it—one bay away—is a double square void that is half inside and half outside. It has no windows on the gallery floor but provides light to below and a double height conservation studio. From the sky, the court reiterates the small square court, though slightly shifted. (see Fig. 8) This court is not only a draw from the lower lobby to the temporary gallery, it also provides the conservation studio with a double height glass wall that faces north. (Fig. 9) In contrast to the water court, the glass here runs across the vault.

The fourth courtyard—the green court—is in the north wing and, again, square. This court occupies the vault and low zones on either side. All four sides are glass. (Fig. 10) With the three contained courts at the gallery level, Kahn is giving us all the possibilities: solid and void, all solid, and all void. (Fig. 11) Acting much like the conservatory court on the lower level, the green court is aligned with the park entrance bay and draws visitors into the galleries. (Fig. 12) The court here is larger and more exposed than the one below because it has to compete with a lot more for attention.

Fig. 9

Fig. 10

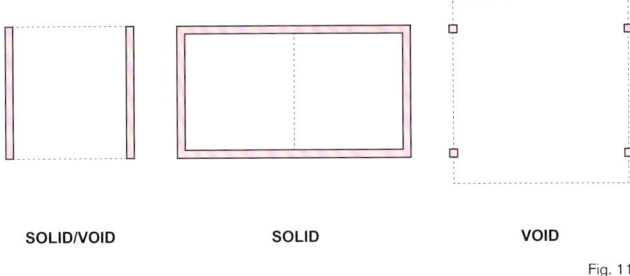

Fig. 11

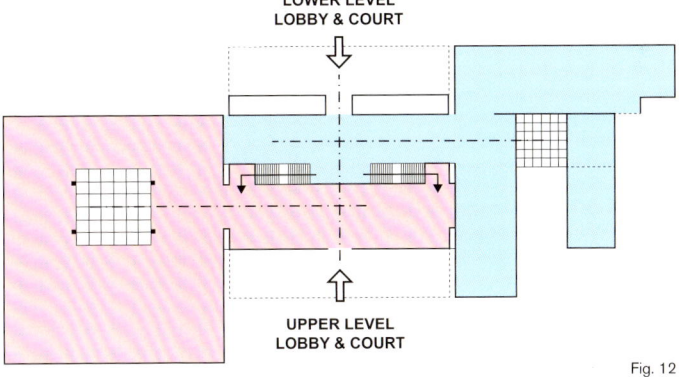

Fig. 12

Kahn is all for squaring up the teams. If there are three contained courtyards at the gallery level (park court, water court, and green court), then there must be three at the lower level. Indeed, there are: the conservatory court and two compressed courts that are trapped between the park porticos and the north and south wings. (Fig. 13) In the slot of the "service zone," these courts provide light for the museum administration and the shipping department through unimpeded glass walls. (Figs. 14, 15)

In addition to the courts in the building, there are two more square courts north and south of the building. Here again, the use of service space and served space makes an appearance. The northern court is the service court and accommodates deliveries while providing for staff parking. Formed by the five-bay north elevation of the museum and a western retaining wall holding back the park, the cuts in the west wall recall the stables at the Villa Madama in Rome with the gardens above. Although this court makes no pretense to be anything but service, it is surprisingly monumentalized: the delivery door is framed in the middle of the five bays and serves as the focus of the court. (Fig. 16)

1. ENTRANCE PORCH 2. ENTRANCE 3. MECHANICAL 4. SHIPPING & RECEIVING
5. ADMINISTRATION 6. CONSERVATOR'S COURT 7. SLOT COURTS

Fig. 13

Fig. 14

Fig. 15

Fig. 16

The southern court—originally identified as a grass theater—is a sculpture court and completely disconnected from the museum. Its only purpose can be to put the museum in the park. Like the carp tank at Villa Lante, the Kimbell sculpture court is isolated and enclosed. However, given all the differences between city, park, delivery, and fire exit, we still find that the building exit is pulled off the stair and centered on a vault. (Fig. 17)

Fig. 17

The elevations continue the theme of mixing service and served. Clearly, the travertine galleries and their exposed structure sit on a concrete base. However, on the street side, the concrete base of the middle pavilion has been lifted to allow entry. (Fig. 18) Though hidden behind the travertine portico walls, a similar action happens in the wings of the west park elevation. (see Fig. 14) If one understands the concrete wall as the edge between city and park, then there is a nice intersection of the two at the gallery floor: the park is pulled to the east edge and the city is pulled to the west edge. By pulling the park through the middle and burying the concrete wall of the wings behind the travertine portico walls, there is a reading of the north and south wings as pavilions. (Fig. 19) Again, this is a similar strategy to what happens at the Villa Lante.

Fig. 18

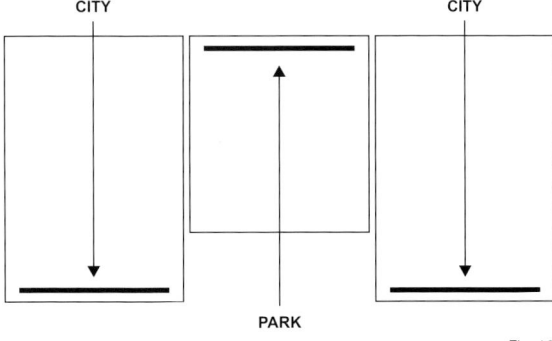

Fig. 19

The lifting of the concrete base allows for the uninterrupted glass walls of the administration offices and shipping department. This is a pure conceit on Kahn's part. The glass wall exists at the edge of these spaces; there is no reason that columns could not have been used to support the gallery walls above. The structural extravagance seems all the more surprising given that the columns on the ground floor are able to shift to accommodate the functions of the spaces: they exist on an edge of the served and service spaces or in the middle of the service space. (see Fig. 13) Therefore, the removal of the columns at the edge must be a declaration of the spanning capacity of concrete and a sop to contemporary technology. Of course, this being Kahn, there is also an alternative reading: that the edge of the museum was once a concrete wall on both levels and that the wall and columns on the lower level were shifted west to create the slot courtyards. There is now an extra advantage, as the columns are used to reinforce the retaining wall.

In addition to the city/park intersection, the long span concrete walls allow for an equivalence between the park gallery entrance and the windows into the service zones at the lower level. Not only does this continue the theme of the intersection of service and served, but the down-up-down of the continuous park glass wall reiterates the out-in-out reading of the portico in the park. (Fig. 20)

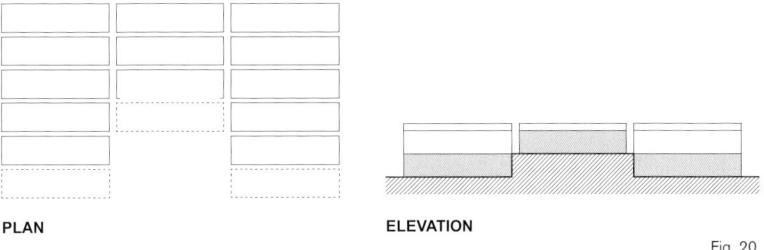

PLAN   ELEVATION

Fig. 20

Returning to the city entrance, one must note that the floor is removed at the porch. (Fig. 21) It would appear that when the concrete wall was raised, it took its floor with it, pushing the first floor up to become a mezzanine level in the library. (Fig. 22) This action is just the beginning of a series of maneuvers that allow for varied accommodations under the vaults. As with the variations of the courtyards, many possibilities are expressed. From the galleries to the compressed library, to the auditorium with a dropped floor, to the clerestory of the conservation studio (see Fig. 9), to the open-sided loggias (Fig. 23), one can experience both the singularity and repetitive nature of the vaults. Their fullness and emptiness is on display; their ability to shape and be shaped is present. A subtle but beguiling detail in the park porticos is the gap that is created by dropping the travertine wall to follow the land. (Fig. 24) This keeps the vault at a constant height and emphasizes the accommodating nature of the ground plane and the consistency of the vaults.

Fig. 21

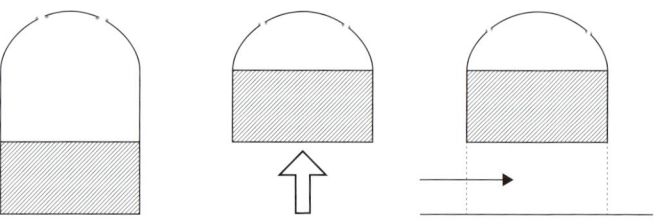

Fig. 22

Fig. 23

Fig. 24

It would appear that Kahn is playing a game of logical consequences. Equivalence and difference are both created by simple actions while retaining the identity of a whole. The density of the library is created by the lifting of the base of the wall at the entry. Likewise, the two missing bays on the garden elevation appear to have been replaced at both the entrance porch and lobby at the lower level, with the compressed bifurcated stair making the connection between the two. (Fig. 25) The openness of the porticos and porch on the park side contrast with the closed nature of the theater, library, and gallery on the city side. (Fig. 26) Each element is defined in terms of another and each element often plays for more than one team.

Understanding both the need for natural light and the damage it can cause paintings, it is interesting to note the subtle but effective ways that Kahn introduces light. In addition to the glass walls of the courtyards and lightwells, it is clear that Kahn was focused on the natural light fixtures that dominate the lighting of the vaults. Light is not allowed to sneak in; it is made present with an apparatus not unlike Aalto's inverted skylights, now more evenly distributed. (see Fig. 2)

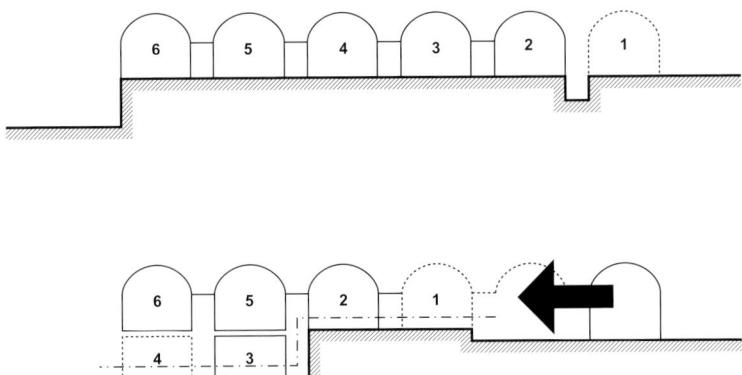

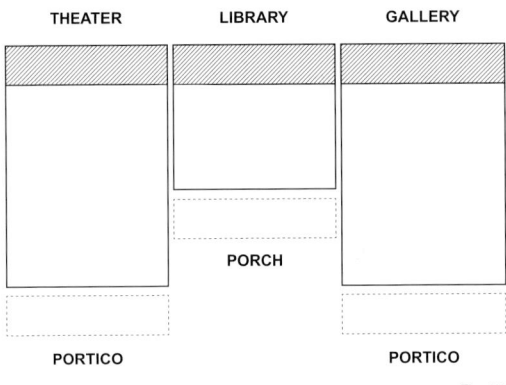

Fig. 25

Fig. 26

There are at least four other "windows." The first is the segmented line that accentuates the shape of the cycloid vault against the elliptical stiffening beam. (Fig. 27) The second is the impossibly narrow strip window that separates the structure of the long span wall from the long span vault in the library. (Fig. 28) The third is the large thermal windows at either end of the library mezzanine and the green court. (see Fig. 10) Finally—and perhaps necessary to articulate the separation of the railroad car vaults—are the vertical slot windows. (see Fig. 21)

Fig. 27

Fig. 28

PRIMORDIAL PRESENCE 101

Elaborated primordial elements are the theme of the Kimbell Art Museum. On the outside, everything is taut. On the inside, everything is sparring for space. Materials are elaborated: concrete, glass, travertine, and wood are put to work, and each has various roles to play. The concrete is clearly working as structure but comes in different forms: column, slab, vault. Travertine is always infill or applied; it is sometimes horizontal and sometimes vertical. Wood is infill or furniture. Applied lead on the roof is the only material with a solitary role: reflecting the clouds. The materials are simple in their essence but rich in their variation and mix. As with many of his buildings, Kahn's selective palette of rough and refined materials here makes the building elegant, but also allows for a comingled reading of Roman baths and rail yards, with chateau elements between them. (Fig. 29)

Fig. 29

Fig. 1

WHIRRING BITS:
CHAREAU'S MAISON DE VERRE

"We live for the most part within enclosed spaces. These form the environment from which our culture grows. Our culture is in a sense a product of our architecture. If we wish to raise our culture to a higher level, we are forced for better or worse to transform our architecture."

- Paul Scheerbart

Maison de Verre is an infill project under an existing building. The house's car court facade is out of context and out of scale. (Fig. 1) The primary facade is glass on the first floor and glass block above. The wrap around the corner is made of the same materials, but in a more accommodating and less abstract manner. The facade announces all of the games that will be played: a distinction between public and private, a utopian projection of industrialized standardization, the illusion and actuality of mobility, and the making of a machine for living. (Fig. 2)

The facade is a complex assemblage pushed into a corner. The projection of the main facade and service wing into the courtyard, the grid of glass blocks, the constant height of the coping, the vertical strips of concrete at the ends of the main and service facades, and the recess in the service wing on the first floor all support the argument that the facade is a single entity bent around a corner. The length of the recess on the service wing is the same as the width of the stair to the apartment in the existing building, indicating that the stair propagated the push to the corner. (Fig. 3)

The horizontal windows in the service wing indicate that the block is subservient to the primary facade. If the windows are understood as tracks, then perhaps the facade has been pulled out from the main volume. The plan supports this idea: on the first floor, the service wing is the same size as the service foyer and could easily be stored there. How it got to be where it is seems to be established by the equivalence between the service wing and the stair and stoop to the upper apartment: the service wing projects from the main facade the same length that the stair and its landing do from the existing building. (Fig. 4)

Like the service wing, the main facade also provides the illusion of movement. The light stanchions in front of the facade and the horizontal rails that connect them back to the house suggest that the main glass block and metal facade can slide in and out from under the existing building. An indication that the facade has been pushed into the frontcourt is that the doctor's study has been pulled away from the garden facade by the same dimension that the primary glass block facade has been projected into the front court. The first-floor void on the service wing suggests that the main facade could be pushed out further.

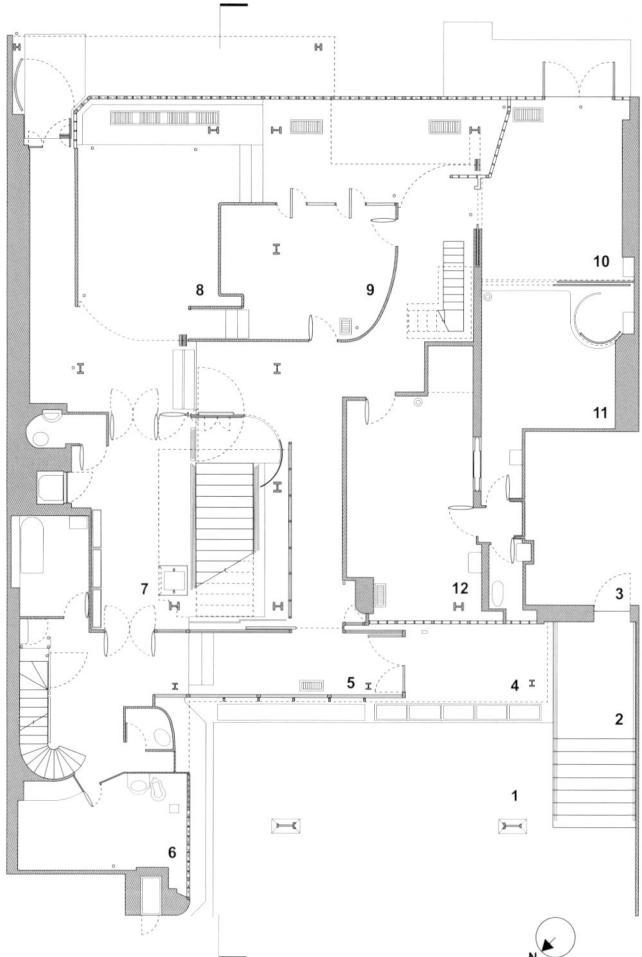

FIRST FLOOR

1. CAR COURT 2. STOOP TO UPPER APARTMENT 3. UPPER APARTMENT ENTRY
4. PORCH 5. VESTIBULE 6. MAID 7. SERVICE ROOM 8. WAITING 9. RECEPTION
10. DOCTOR'S CONSULT ROOM 11. EXAM ROOM 12. SURGERY ROOM

Fig. 2

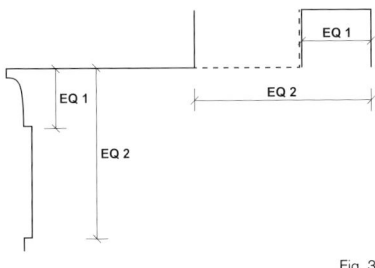

Fig. 3

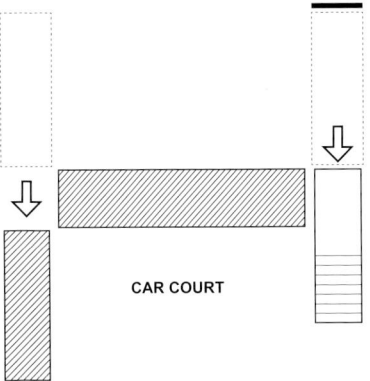

CAR COURT

Fig. 4

The house comes across as a large Chinese puzzle with pieces that have been shifted to create a variety of spaces. At a smaller scale, the movement becomes more refined. According to five of the bays of voided glass block frames on the first floor, the corner is not bent. Rather, the main facade is stable and the vestibule has slid to the side to create a void that becomes the front porch. (Fig. 5) Further, it would seem that the glass vestibule, which is the same length of the main facade, has been pushed into the service wing and then recoiled. In the process of recoiling, it has projected a small pavilion onto the recessed front porch. (Fig. 6) The object aspect of the pavilion is made clear because—unlike the rest of the glass vestibule—the small projected element is neither veiled by the glass block frame nor shielded by the plantings. There is also a strange pairing or shifting: five pavers sit in front of the four-module porch while the four-bay planter sits in front of the five-bay vestibule. (Fig. 7)

The movement does not just exist in the horizontal plane; it is equally prevalent in the facade. The voided glass block frames in front of the glass wall not only support the idea that the main facade is momentarily fixed and that the service wing has slid out from the house, it also ties the upper glass block facade to the ground via the framing. The glass block has merely been removed. The lacy frame functions as a trellis for the planter below and as a veil for the vestibule of this new world. (see Fig. 6)

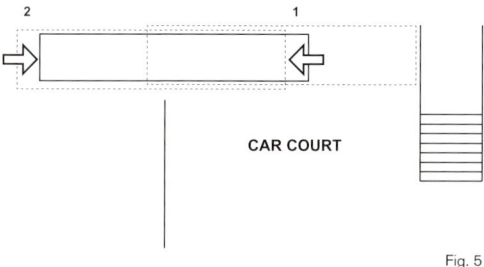

Fig. 5

Fig. 6

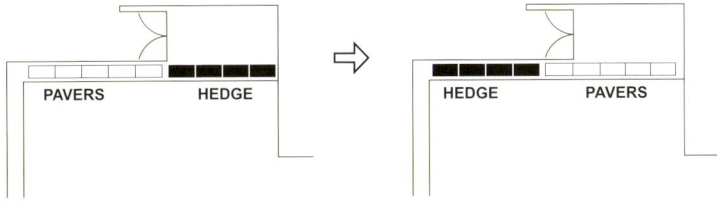

Fig. 7

Above the porch, there is a thick black beam that suggests that the glass-block grid has been raised and stacked in the thickened band. (see Fig. 6) However, if the black beam is read as primary, then it is equally possible to read the main glass block facade as having once been aligned with the glass block wall at the rear of the porch. The high windows in the recessed facade support both interpretations. In the scenario where it is pushed *up*, the windows trace the push of the porch soffit. In the scenario where the windows are pushed *back*, they reiterate the infill capacity of the frame. Another detail indicating a vertical shift is the half-buried column that presents the front door chimes. (Fig. 8) This column can be understood as having either been pushed up from the ground and then retracted or as having once been aligned with the windows above and now lowered for convenience.

Fig. 8

The garden facade is another Chinese puzzle or mechanized collage: a form of synthetic cubism at its best. The composition suggests stacked metro cars. Elements such as a projected slab, a glass block wall, lights, and strip windows have been slid into place. (Fig. 9) The third floor terrace slab is particularly emphatic about its presence. One possibility for this emphasis is that the slab has been projected into the garden as a horizontal plane, similar to the way that the salon volume is projected into the front car court.

Fig. 9

Another possibility is that the slab is indicative of a real ground plane and the Paris metro is revealed below. The strip window on the ground floor and the projected concrete slab above represent the original length of a metro car before it crashed into the garden wall, causing it to pile up through the ground plane. At the terrace level, there are four metro car panels facing the garden from the master bedroom and bits of the metro car have been scattered along the glass block wall. Looking at the elevation, if the metro cars are moving to the right then the terrace slab is moving to the left. The whole of the garden facade is in flux.

The theme of *parts in motion* continues upon entering the house from the vestibule through the sliding door. The thinness of the entry hall compared with the breadth of the vestibule is tangible. (see Fig. 2) Examining the plan, it is evident that the imposition of the upper apartment stair has pushed the doctor's surgery room into the middle of the building, making the entrance hall into a corridor and pushing the house stair against the service room. (Fig. 10) To offset the squeezing, the transparent glass wall of the house stair provides some relief, but one is compelled to go deep into the building in order to enter either the house or the office.

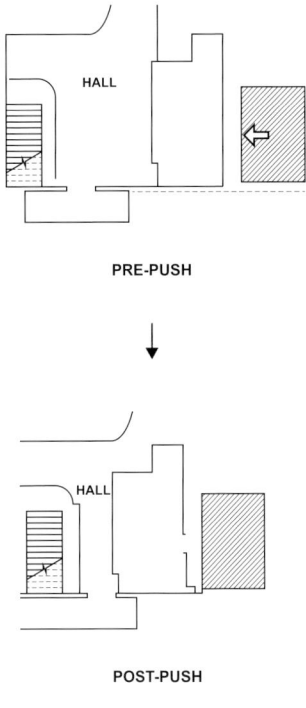

Fig. 10

The house stair is interesting for several reasons. (Fig. 11) First is the way that it descends to a floating landing on the first floor. Second is the manner in which it is constructed with open risers and side rails. Though not mechanically operable, it reads as a retractable stair lowered only to receive guests. Third, the double height volume of the stair has been compressed as the stair hall has been pushed into the service room, rendering the service space and served space as equals (and perhaps constituting a statement about the democratization of the service component). (Fig. 12) The fact that the stair has been pushed to the edge of the service room is confirmed by the cut of the stair landing in the salon (Fig. 13), and the landing itself traces the fact that the stair hall was at one time more central. The idea of the stair having been centered is reinforced by the fact that the landing is extended by the same dimension as the imposition of the apartment stair.

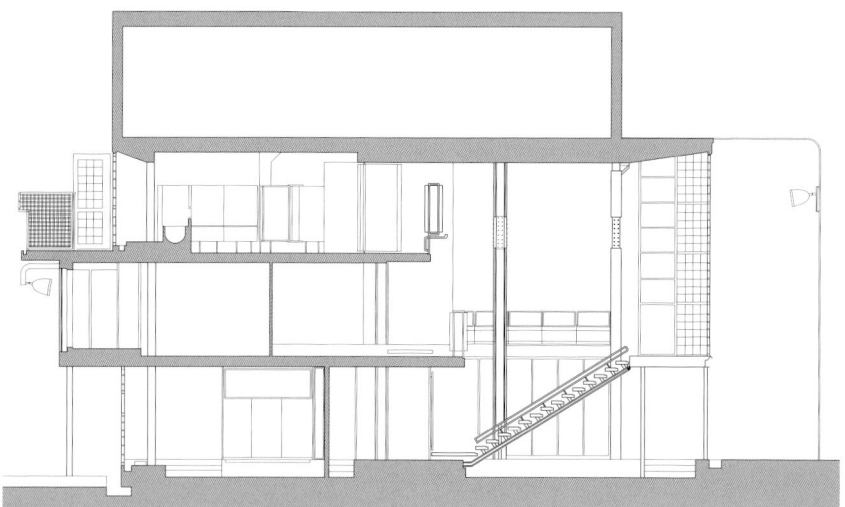

Fig. 11

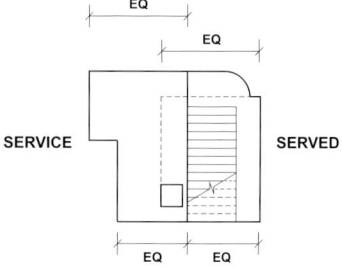

Fig. 12

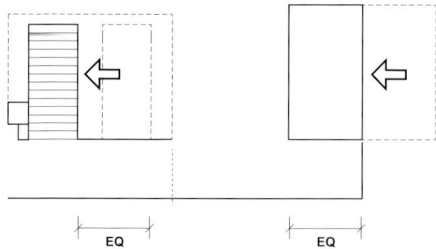

Fig. 13

If the entrance hall and the stair are pushed to one side, then the doctor's suite arrayed along the garden facade is organized and pushed in the opposite direction. (see Fig. 2) The narrow passage to the receptionist's office from the waiting area makes it appear as if the room has been moved or compressed. The curved wall on one side of the room is another indication of the adjacent forces. The stair to the doctor's study above suffers the effects of the imposition of the apartment stair. Finally, there is the glass block wall that has been pushed into the doctor's consulting room. (Fig. 14)

Fig. 14

If on the first floor there was any doubt about parts being in motion, then the second floor could not be more overt about it. (Fig. 15) As on the first floor, there is shifting from side to side. The primary stair landing projects into the main salon and leaves a trace of the stair's former location in the main salon. The stair to the upper apartment shifts into and compresses the salon. The library shelves that wrap around the corner support the impact of the apartment stair. In addition, the apartment stair has shifted the columns, setting up an axis from the middle bedroom door to the front facade. If the apartment stair were to be pushed back out of the space, there would be a consistent span between the two freestanding columns and the column next to the shelving. (Fig. 16) In the vertical direction, the columns appear to stretch upwards with what could rightly be referred to as column spacers: heavily riveted and painted orange on the outside of the flange. (Fig. 17)

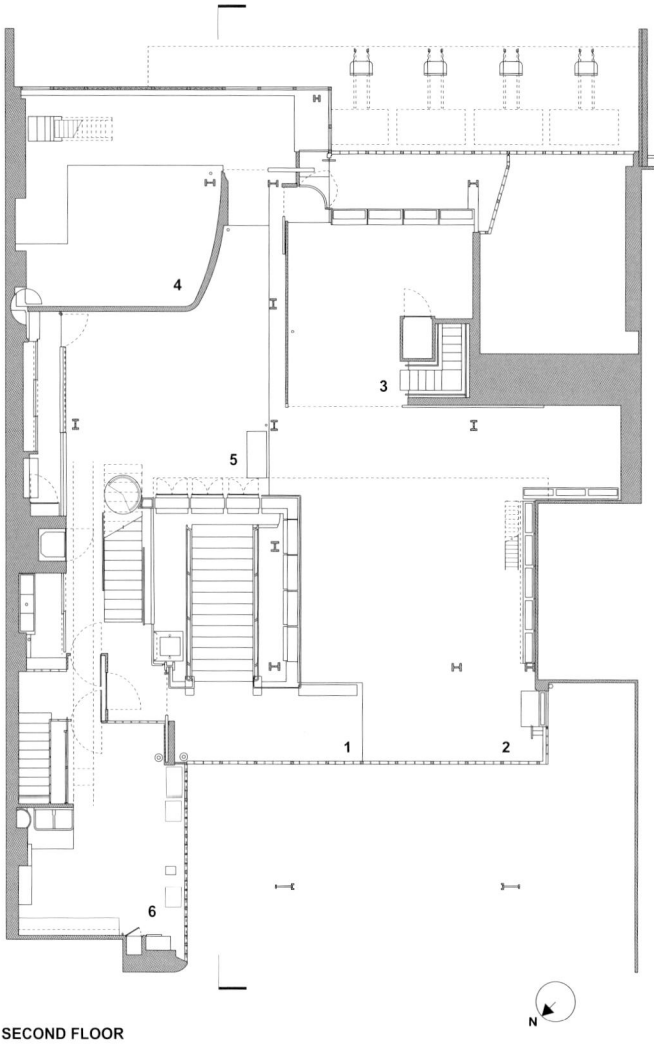

SECOND FLOOR

1. STAIR LANDING 2. SALON 3. DOCTOR'S STUDY 4. DAY ROOM 5. DINING 6. KITCHEN

Fig. 15

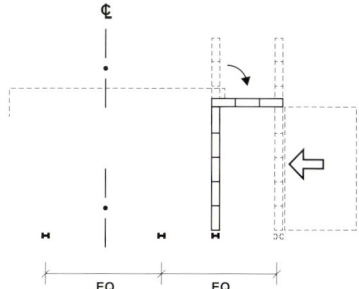

Fig. 16

Fig. 17

The doctor's study is a complex record of motions, one generated by a solid form and the other created by a void. The edge of the tiling in the dining room indicates that the study has been pushed into the salon, either from the side or from the garden. From the side, the thick bar with the study stair at its end appears to have rammed the study sideways. From the garden, the study wall seems to be moving forward, tethered to the garden wall by the angled glass block wall of the doctor's consulting room. The bookcases along the void are more edging that helps recall the extent of the former salon. The void between the garden facade and the study is the ying to the yang of the dayroom projection into the garden. (see Fig. 15)

On the third floor, the shifting continues. (Fig. 18) This is most notable in the void of the salon that has been pushed into the house, causing the bedroom corridor bookshelves and storage unit modules to bend around the salon. The ten modules along the bedroom corridor clearly align with the ten modules of the front court facade. The

15 modules (including the elevator) once indicated the width of the house from the apartment stair to the neighbors' wall; now they frame the salon. (Figs. 18 & 19) On the other side of the bedroom corridor, the wardrobe units that once matched the 10 units that face the salon shift to allow entrance to the bedrooms. The result is three sets of three closets, with an additional closet splayed against the master water closet. (Fig. 20) Somewhat more apparent is the shifting of the bedroom walls. The wardrobe

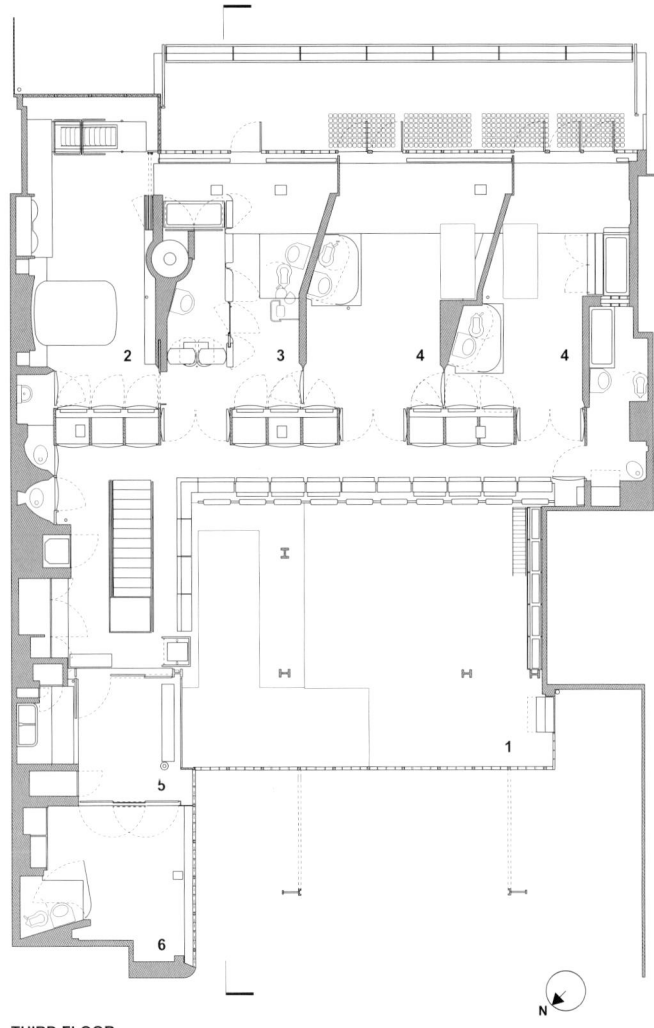

THIRD FLOOR

1. VOID 2. MASTER BEDROOM 3. MASTER BATH 4. BEDROOM 5. SERVICE 6. MAID

Fig. 18

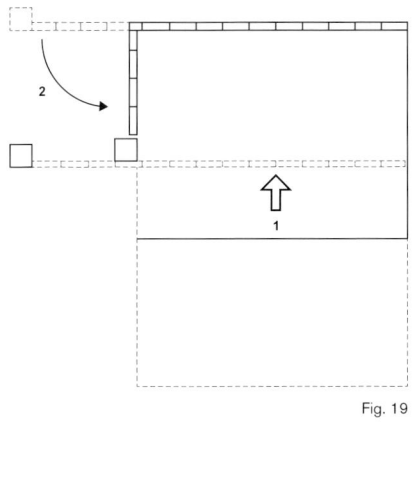

Fig. 19

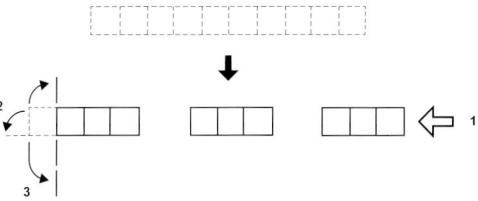

Fig. 20

units on the hall wall and the imposition of the guest bathroom suggest that they have been pushed toward the master bedroom. The columns suggest that they have been pushed in the opposite direction.

All the shifting has created numerous L-shaped forms that exist in plan, section, elevation, as solid, or as void. In a Beaux Arts building, each room would be discrete. Here, everything is in motion in the form of overlaps, impositions, compression, and expansion. From the building being pushed into the corner of the car court to the stacked metro cars, and from the configuration of the third floor to the shape of essentially every room, the L-shaped configurations work in many ways. These configurations imply movement and suggest larger diaphanous spaces. Each of these instances is a useful device to indicate early 20th-century optimism. The implied movement denies stasis and suggests a machine in service to a better life. These expanded spaces can be seen as an abundance and indicative of the benefits of industrialization. The lightly contained spaces kill poche and reveal material diversity and the reality of elements both inside and out.

There are several ways to form an "L." (Fig. 21) It can be a bent bar made up of two elements or a series of elements that come together. It can be created by different rates of expansion or contraction on one side of a bar. A rectangle can have hard and soft sides, allowing for plasticity. Overlapping spaces can form an L. A rectangle can have a corner cut out of it to form an L, or corner object can be inserted to do the same.

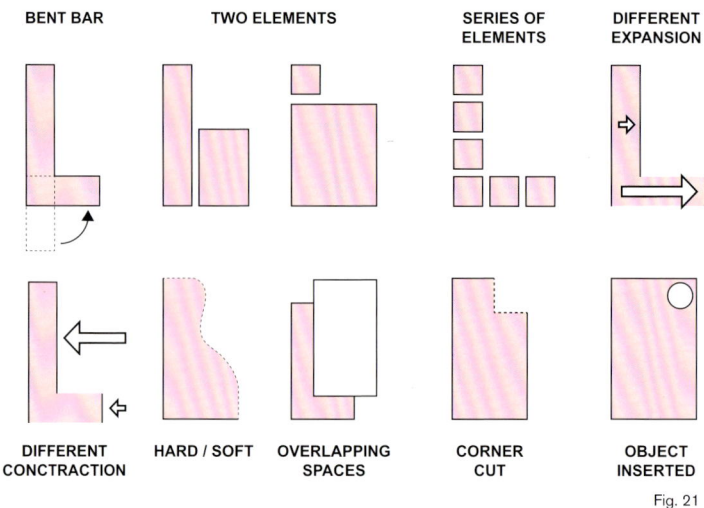

Fig. 21

In Maison de Verre, the bent L's can be found in the glass block of the entry sequence, in the recessed spaces facing the car court on the first floor, and in the entry hall that wraps around the house stair. They can be found in the curved corner of the receptionist's office and the compressed stair to the doctor's study. They can be found in the bookcases that edge the salon and the raised floor in the day room.

As for the subtraction of elements to form an L, the freestanding double height columns in the salon are an obvious example, where a column has been removed or relocated to form the L. (Fig. 22) As has been mentioned, the span between column D (next to the shelves) and column C appears to have been shortened by the imposition of the apartment stair. If the apartment stair were retracted, the spans between columns B and C would be the same as the span between columns C and D. The importance of this articulation is made apparent by the fact that column C has been slightly shifted to produce equal spans between columns. (see Fig. 16) In addition, the turning of column A allows one to read the L as an addition: a line plus an object. The alternating location of the column extenders along the height of the individual columns seems to indicate that columns A and B are one pair, while columns C and D are another. (see Fig. 17)

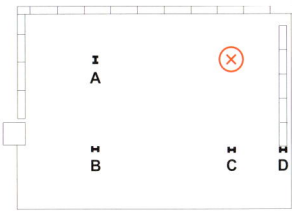

Fig. 22

An L created by removing part of a rectangle is most apparent with the glass block wall in the doctor's consulting room and the imposition of the stair and phone booth in the corner of the doctor's study. (see Fig. 15) L's made by inserting an object in the corner of a rectangle are most clear in the changing room of the doctor's examination room (see Fig. 2) and the addition of the washing units in the bedrooms. (see Fig. 18) L's created by the overlapping of spaces are most clear when the dayroom pushes into the dining room or the doctor's study pushes into the salon.

The L's also exist in section. The house stair and its connection to the salon is the first to be encountered. (Fig. 23) The doctor's foyer and its relationship to the study is the second. (Fig. 24) Perhaps a bit more complex, the dayroom and the master bedroom form an L with the connection made by the retractable stair. (Fig. 25) On the garden facade, the stacked metro cars form a clear L and the glass block wall below the bedroom terrace articulates the sectional extent of the doctor's office, forming an L with the doctor's study. (see Fig. 9)

The platforms found in multiple rooms are subtle, but they trace spatial and visual connections that embody the sectional L's found elsewhere. On the ground floor, L's are formed by the raised stair and the lowered waiting room and service space. On the second floor, the lowering of the stair landing is most notable, but the ledges in the dining room and dayroom also present L's as changes in section. On the third floor, the ledges and beds in all of the bedrooms do the same.

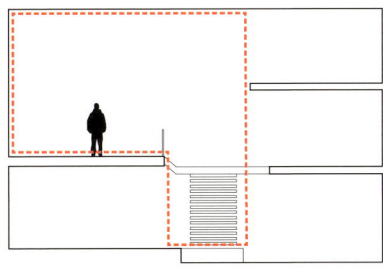

Fig. 23

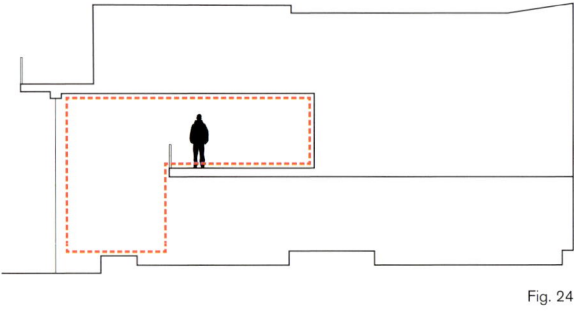

Fig. 24

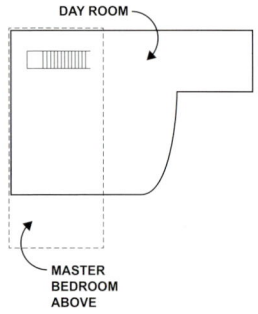

Fig. 25

The elements of the house are not limited to the illusion and tracing of movement; things actually do move. On the first floor, there is the sliding interior front door, the curved door to the house stair (and its screening device) (Fig. 26), the sliding door that connects the doctor's consulting room to the examination room, the curved sliding door on the changing cubical, and the curved garden gate. On the second floor, operable elements include the louvers in the grand salon (Fig. 27), the wheel that operates the study windows (Fig. 28), the sliding doors in the dining room, the industrial door between the study and the salon, the mobile library steps, the horizontal dumbwaiter from the kitchen to the dining room (Fig. 29), and the rotating door to the storage cabinet in the dining room. On the third floor, moving (or movable) elements exist in the form of cupboards, closets, water closets, and wash rooms.

Clearly this mechanization is meant to lead to a better and more hygienic life. The intervening space is filled with modular bookracks on which storage units are superimposed, wardrobe units that open into the bedrooms and bathrooms, swivel storage units in the master bathroom (Fig. 30), operable perforated metal screens that contain the swiveling bidets and sink units in the bedrooms (Fig. 31), and the retractable stair between the master bedroom and the dayroom below. (Fig. 32) Like a giant Chinese puzzle, most of these elements require at least two actions to access them.

Fig. 26

Fig. 27

Fig. 28

Fig. 29

Fig. 30

Fig. 31

Chareau was a furniture designer. His refined industrial aesthetic can also be seen in the stairs to the doctor's study (Fig. 33), the bookcases and cupboards that line the salon, and the furniture that he designed specifically for the house. Although primarily made of metal, they share traits with the 19th-century crafts movement and present themselves as refinements of the heavier and more overwrought industrial aesthetic of the gear mechanisms that open and close the operable windows, doors, and ventilation elements that appear elsewhere. The difference can be understood as a distinction between public and private spaces and the elements that occupy them.

Fig. 32

Maison de Verre is modular and made of reproducible industrial bits. This is certainly true for the glass block, which is gathered together in four-block-wide and six-block-high module panels. In plan, this module is repeated a number of times throughout the public spaces: in the glass block walls, in the bookcases, in the wardrobes, in the metro car panels, and in the windows. In elevation, there are slight variations. For instance, the metro car panels are the equivalent of eight blocks high while the storage units hung on the bookcases are five blocks high. The windows show up in four sizes: two-block tall, three-block tall, four-block tall, and floor-to-ceiling. There is the illusion

Fig. 33

WHIRRING BITS **123**

of industrialization because the elements are metal, precise in their application, and seemingly reproducible. Yet, they are intricate, iterated, and particular to their purpose, location, and effect.

The bookcases and storage units lining the salon are a good example of this iterability. They are between one and 14 shelves high, made of solid or perforated metal, with or without backs, and sometimes replaced with wooden cupboards. The stairs also iterate. The theme is announced in the front courtyard with the light stand ladders that exist in contrast with the upper apartment porch. The lighting brackets could not be more spare or efficient. Inside the house, the solid service stair contrasts with the doctor's thin tube study stair. The open main stair exists in opposition to the folded plate second-floor stair or master bedroom's retractable stair. The stairs iterate in scale, materiality, and presence, but also in hierarchy: from house, to service, to doctor, to the doctor's wife.

Finally, the issue of public versus private is iterated. The theme presents itself immediately on the primary facade with the glass walls of the ground floor and the translucent glass block above. What happens in that translucent space is a mystery. The front door chime presents the choices of doctor, visitor, and service. (see Fig. 8) Service is immediately dispatched, with one being directed to the service stair from the vestibule before entering the house or doctor's office. Visitors to the house are required to open a veiled glass door to the main stair.

Upon entering the living quarters, the salon is now the public space in the house while the dining room and the doctor's study are ancillary. Service space is hidden behind a metal facade, a service elevator, and a screened stair to the third floor. The day room is the most private space on the floor, with a small passage to the doctor's study and a retractable stair to the master bedroom. It is worth noting the difference between the main stair (open to the salon) and the stair to the bedrooms (open to the service corridor but screened from the salon). Along one wall of the bedrooms, the corridor is also screened from the salon, sometimes with solid panels and sometimes with perforated metal. (Fig. 34) The storage units that separate the bedrooms from the corridor act as a service-and-served barrier, able to be loaded by the staff from the corridor and opened by the family from within the bedrooms. In the bedrooms, the privacy of the washing units is made emphatic with their perforated metal screens.

Despite alternative readings, Maison de Verre came into being in a time of turmoil. New technologies were changing the world and industrial production promised plenty for everyone. This is a house caught between the old and the new. The inclusion of the doctor's office in the house, the presence of servants' quarters, the furniture, and the careful craftsmanship are clearly indicative of the 19th century. The industrial aesthetic, the thinness of the walls, the infusion of light, the mechanization of the elements, and the reproducible components all represent the new. The illusion and reality of mobility is undeniable, and if one understands the elaboration of the reproducible elements as one kind of action, then iteration is another form of action. All of the elements in the house affect each other. Everywhere, one finds the development of elements for modern life, pieced together in a complex collection. From the modulated and articulated elements to the literal image of industrial bits, one can almost hear the whirring of a machine for living.

Fig. 34

Fig. 1

GULP:
HAWKSMOOR'S ST. GEORGE'S BLOOMSBURY

"It is a work that has a kind of simplicity, ease, and density of detail that only a film-maker in total command of his craft can bring off, and then only rarely."

- Vincent Canby

There is little question that Nicholas Hawksmoor's St. George's Bloomsbury is considered a masterpiece. (Fig. 1) Begun in 1716 and completed in 1731, it has recently been restored to its original state, making it ripe for review.

Notwithstanding its significance to architectural history, St. George's represents a formidable command of craft. It is a game of logical consequences in which Hawksmoor uses program and context (both physical and cultural) as muses to manipulate the very stuff of architecture. Though it plays out in classical garb, it remains relevant to contemporary discourse. A cornice, for present purposes, is just another name for a horizontal line. (Fig. 2)

Fig. 2

St. George's is a pile of classical references and the intersection of church and state—of the sacred and profane. The obvious combination of a steeple church and classical temple is well known, but it is the canny inventiveness with which the two buildings are merged that makes it noteworthy.

At the most basic level, the church is composed of three elements: steeple, hall, and apse. (Fig. 3) Hinting at the complexities to come, the temple is composed of three gabled pieces with temple fronts at either end of a higher, central mass. (Fig. 4) Reading the hall as a temple, we notice its orientation along a civic axis from south to north. It's a composition of columns and thin walls, and the fragmentary, horizontal, and extended character of its elements. The church intersects the temple along a perpendicular liturgical axis from west to east, or steeple to apse, and is composed of arched forms, thick walls, and vertical, compressed elements. (Figs. 5 & 6)

Both the church and the temple have stacked windows and share the central space. However, the windows on the south and north elevations are more narrowly spaced than their counterparts on the west and east elevations. (Fig. 7) This also gives the impression that the temple windows are spreading apart and that those of the church are subject to a contrasting compression. Though the cubic volume of the central space suggests an equivalence between church and temple, the strong contrast between their elements—thick, arched, windowed, and vertical church walls versus thin, columned, open, and horizontal temple walls—makes their differences abundantly clear.

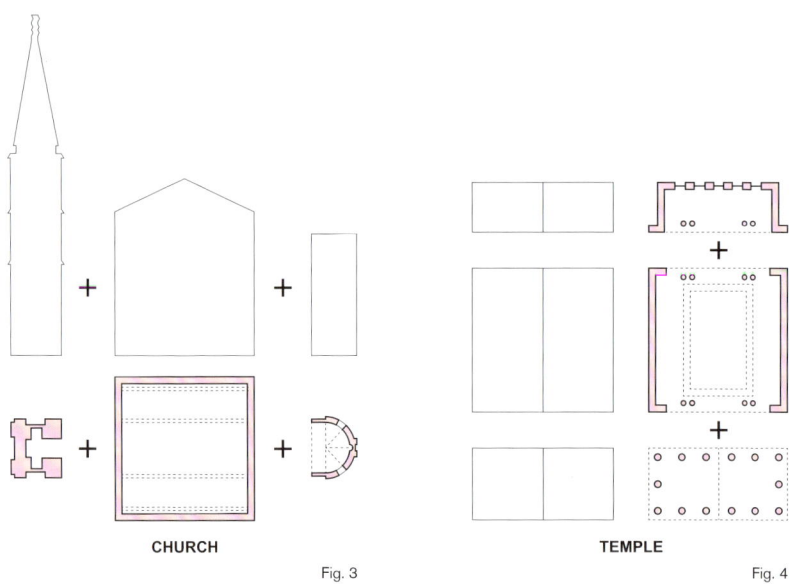

CHURCH   TEMPLE

Fig. 3   Fig. 4

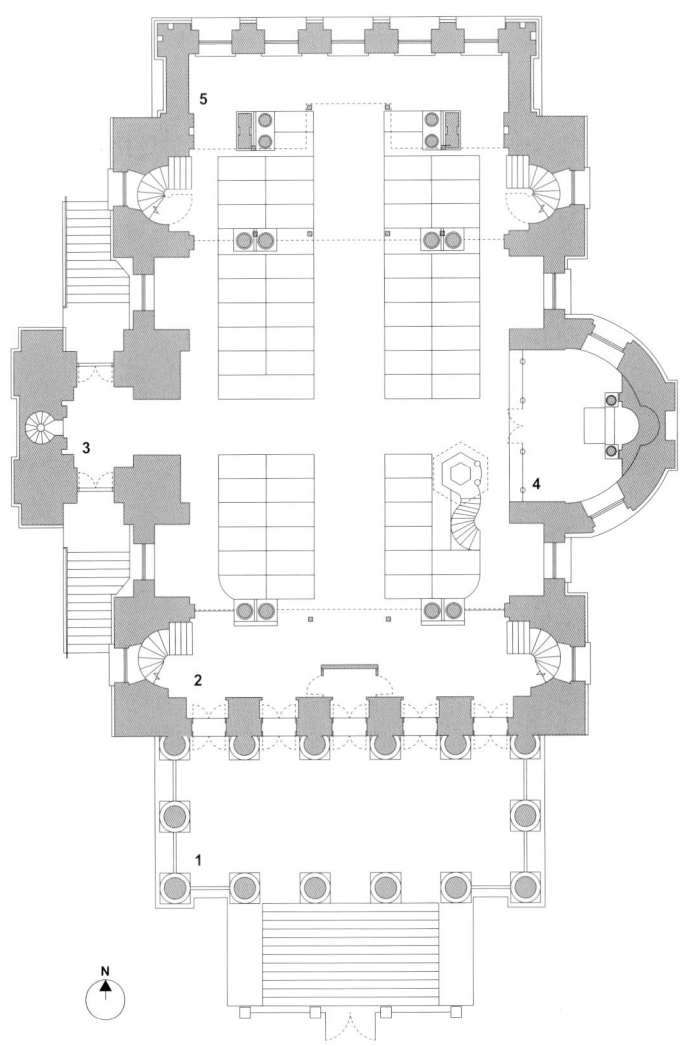

1. PORCH 2. SANCTUARY 3. ENTRY 4. APSE 5. PARISH HALL

Fig. 5

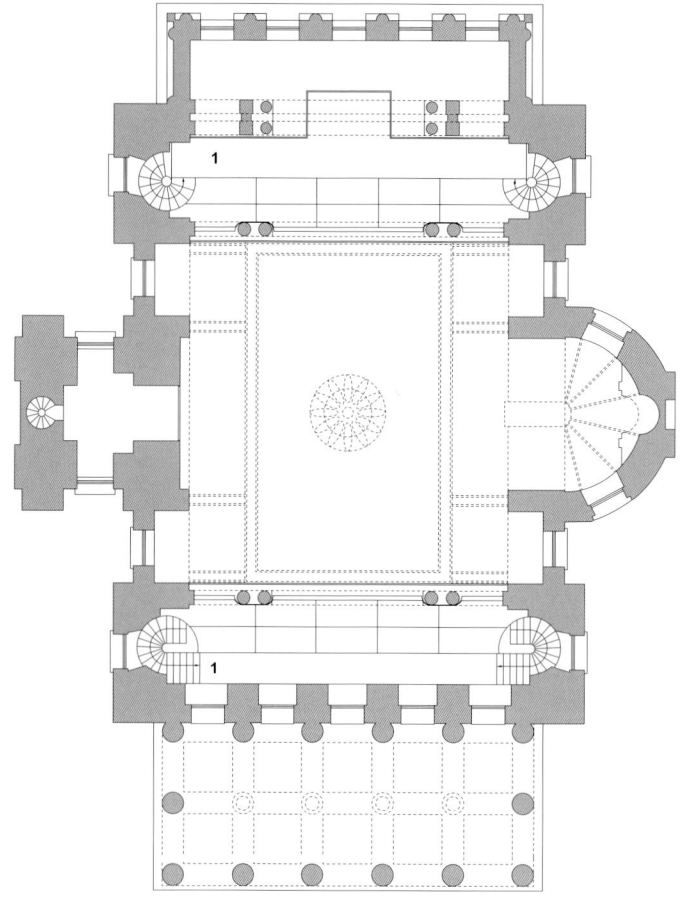

1. GALLERY

Fig. 6

Fig. 7

The depressed arches on all four sides of the central space further underscore the ambiguity. One way to understand the west arch is that it is filled by the side wall of the temple and layered with the temple's horizontal lines. (Fig. 8) Yet the stacked arched openings indicate that the wall could just as easily be understood as part of the church steeple. The subtle differences in the arches create hierarchy within the space. If we understand the north and south arches as the norm, then the east arch that bounds the chancel is double the thickness and the west arch is one half their depth. Together, they mark the progression from west to east and call attention to the chancel arch as the most important in the space.

Fig. 8

A reading of the central space as part of the church is supported by the presence of tall, deep arches on the east and west walls that act as aisles on either side of the depressed nave arches. The Palladian recesses in the clerestory are not only a sop to the English classicists of the time, they also reiterate a nave with side aisles. (see Figs. 7 & 8) The entablature running between the depressed central arches and the tall side arches on the west and east elevations further evoke this idea, though it is the galleries adjacent to the tall arches that in fact define the profile of the central volume and are the actual side aisles.

The clerestory windows support readings that suggest both the extension of the temple and the compression of the church. They appear to have been pulled north and south with the galleries as well as bent around the corners on the east and west elevations (Figs. 9 & 10), suggesting that the nave was once longer but is now compressed in order to fit the narrow site. Further, if one reads the outer church wall as the temple's cella wall that defines the space, then both the tower and the apse appear to have been pushed into the center space. (Fig. 11)

Fig. 9

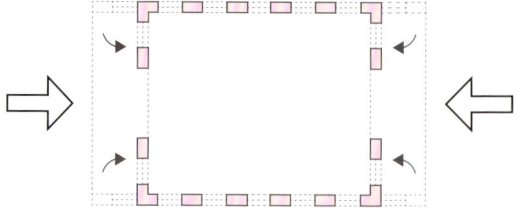

Fig. 10

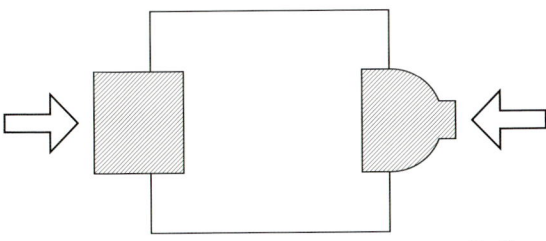

Fig. 11

An alternate reading of these pieces allows us to consider St. George's as composed of discrete elements (tower, apse, and side galleries) added to a central space. Each of these added pieces is thick-walled and vaulted. None of them sit under the gabled roofs of the temple and all are tied together by a heavy cornice on the outside. (Fig. 12 & see Fig. 2) One can imagine the apse and the tower as elaborations on the simpler gallery elements: the apse as the outer layer of a double wall has been bent around itself and inserted into the opening of the inner layer (Fig. 13) and the tower mass as a thick wall has been spread apart and carries with it the other wall past the east-facing arch. (Fig. 14)

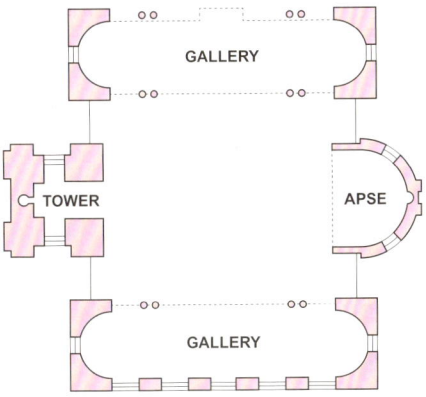

Fig. 12

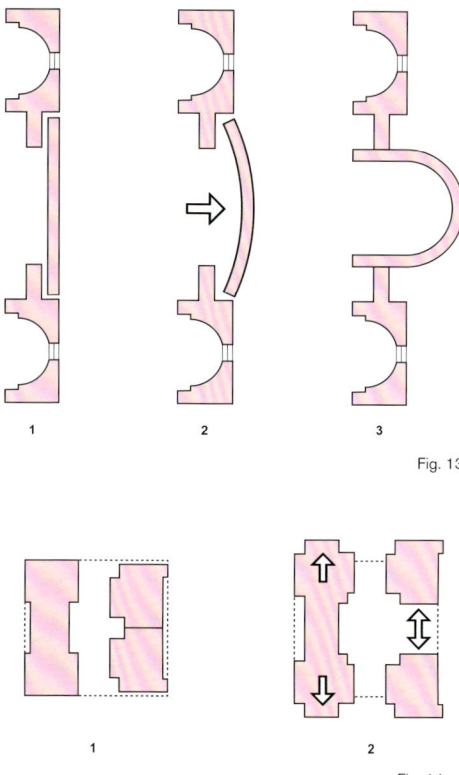

Fig. 13

Fig. 14

The height of the central space is a result of either an upward expansion of the temple or the compression of the church. On the south-north axis, the expansion of the temple recalls the lid of a jack-in-the-box. It is easy to imagine that the demi-lune in the tympanum held the latch that was released. Along the west-east axis, it appears that the compression of the outer walls has forced the center upward. (Fig. 15) In this case, compression is registered in the gable of the roof, as if the once-flat roof of the church had pitched upward to become part of the temple. Again, the wrap of the clerestory windows confirms the reading of compression.

On the east and west elevations of the central space, the thick piers are unarticulated from the floor to the entablature. (Fig. 16) The north and south elevations are made predominantly horizontal by cutting across the vertical openings with the wooden galleries, by placing the columns on bases, and by extending the bases, horizontal moldings, and entablatures into the deep arches (i.e., side aisles) of the church. (Fig. 17) As entablature to the columns and capitals to the piers, the cornice and the interlace molding above tie the ensemble back together. (see Fig. 8)

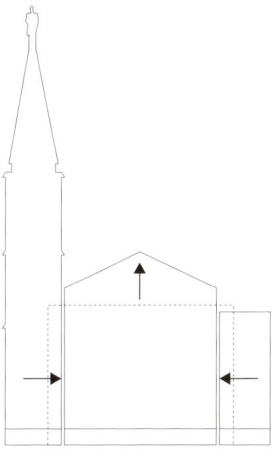

Fig. 15

Fig. 16

Fig. 17

Coupled columns help to form the primary and side aisles within the central space, but their grouping also indicates the expansive nature of the temple. They appear to have been pushed or pulled out of the middle of the elevations to argue for equivalence between temple and church. Above, the temple ceiling molding somewhat obscures the church molding by using it as a track along which its shape changes from a square to a rectangle. (Figs. 18 & 19)

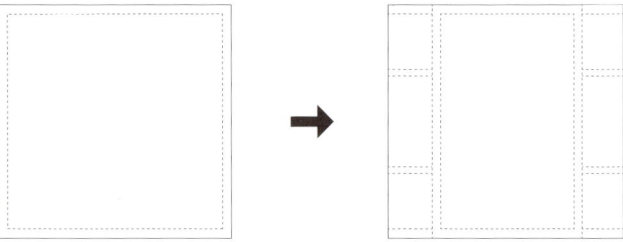

Fig. 18

Fig. 19

Hawksmoor exploited the dialogue between church and temple processions for all it was worth; both forms share the central hall. The church procession is liturgical, beginning in the tower and ending at the altar in the apse. The temple procession is civic. It begins at the portico and ends in the parish hall. The portico is a grand civic statement: on the street and open. The church tower is more removed: down the alley and closed.

The end spaces are most revealing. In the church sequence, the importance of the apse is made clear through its manifestation as compressed, deep, dark, thick-walled, and subtractive. The termination of the temple sequence is more complicated: it is an interiorized version of the portico. (Fig. 20) The space is extended, shallow, brightly lit, thin-walled, and additive. The projected mezzanine gallery, the double arch ensemble, and the narrowly spaced windows all work in contrast to the apse.

Fig. 20

The projected gallery acts as an exedra: a possible termination to the axial sequence that places the parish hall beyond the space of the church proper. It also diminishes the importance of the axis and highlights the lateral quality of the parish hall by placing the temple axis in a low, shaded space while highlighting the last of two sets of paired columns along the axis. The round columns are paired north and south in contrast to the east and west pairing of those adjacent to the central space. These columns appear to have been turned 90 degrees off the temple axis to contrast with the lateral axis of the parish hall. It is this lateral quality that most emphatically argues that the parish hall is outside the church. The square piers that back up the round paired columns clear the wide processional space of the temple axis while the paired columns themselves perform a clever perspectival trick. Viewed from the central space, they could reasonably be mistaken for being spaced farther apart than they are. Based on this illusion, the parish hall appears even farther away than it actually is. From the same vantage point it is clear that the parish hall windows are both further removed and closer together than the windows in the gallery/portico wall, resulting in another illusionistic extension of the temple axis.

Both the portico and the parish hall are capped by gabled roofs that appear to be the result of compression along the west-east axis. If the gabled roofs were reassembled into a single form, the result would be a temple that is the same proportion as the deep ceiling molding in the center space. On the exterior, the dentil detailing of the portico and parish hall is more refined than that on the bulk of the building, and the temple's extension is recorded in both the 3/4-exposed columns of the portico (Fig. 21) and in the vestigial columns that emerge at the intersection of the church gallery and the wall of the parish hall. (Fig. 22) Continuing the distinction between temple and church, the temple elements have flat ceilings with moldings in contrast to the church galleries that are vaulted. However, since they also play a secondary role as spacers within the expanded temple volume, the galleries also have fragments of flat ceilings. (Fig. 23)

Fig. 21

Fig. 22

On the building's north elevation, the reading of the temple as horizontal, open, columned, and extended becomes even more emphatic. (see Fig. 22) While the incessant interruption of any continuous verticals with capitals, bases, sills, and overlaid string courses all favor a horizontal reading, it is the introduction of the entablature and projected cornice, the strong base, the cornice below the pediment, and the single-story orders that ultimately impose the horizontal reading.

Fig. 23

Still on the exterior, the solid side walls of the parish hall and the columns engaged in the gallery wall further suggest that the temple form has been pulled from or through the gallery. The column pier ensemble and double piers on the east and west walls of the parish hall support the idea that a further northern extension is possible. This is an idea supported on the interior by the two depressed arches and the doubled columns between the gallery and the parish hall. When seen against their singular cousins between the gallery and the central space, they appear poised to slip further to the north.

The north elevation is similarly animated; no two planes align. (see Fig. 22) Keystones with protruding centers project past a string course of alternating depths that hangs well beyond the stone base below. On the first floor, the upper and lower walls, the window surrounds, the engaged pilasters, and the projected sills all occupy different planes. The second floor is recessed behind the first and has double-layered wall window surrounds and columns on different planes. Pulled in front of the second story, the pediment is the most stable element, though its demi-lune projects slightly beyond its otherwise blank tympanum. The effect makes the second floor read as a loggia, open between the columns. It is suggestive of yet another extension of building elements, this time along a ground-to-sky axis.

The second-floor windows sit on the entablature of the first floor. The lack of sills for the windows and the separation of the entablature from the pediment further support the idea that the recessed facade has been pulled up from below. The overscaled keystones also participate in an upward movement, with further vertical movement held in check by the protruding first floor window sills.

Compression and extension are also illustrated on the south elevation at the street. On the west-east axis, it is clear that the classical temple has been affected by some force since its stairs do not go the full width of the portico and the portico is less wide than the building. In Rome, all of these elements would have aligned. The unarticulated wall of the gallery represents the church (smooth and vertical) as well as the possibility of the portico having slid across its surface. The temple stairs are more complicated: they could have been compressed, but perhaps—as the stairs at the tower suggest—they have been cut off and relocated. (see Fig. 1)

The portico columns are pulled forward, almost off the floor of the porch. This move is supported by the rear columns of the portico being three-quarters removed from the wall. If the stair side walls are understood as extensions of the porch floor, then it would seem that, although there has been some movement, the temple has not yet been fully extended.

On the roof there is further evidence of south-north extension. Typically, a classical temple is crowned by a single roof. At St. George's, the roof has been broken into three parts and extended along the south-north axis. A classical temple would have plinths at the corners of the pediment to hold sculptures. Here, the plinths have been extruded to the north, as if they were rails along which the temple facade could slide. (Fig. 24) The south-north stretching and extension can also be tracked in the dimension of the east-west walls and the overt collection of layers on the north facade.

Finally, there is the issue of the temple-church being composed simultaneously of three, five, seven, and nine bays along each axis. The elements can be assembled in many different scenarios. On the west-east axis, the tower, hall, and apse form an easy *A-B-A** arrangement. The stacked windows on the portico and parish hall elevations could not be more clear about a five-bay arrangement. The side walls of the portico, the wrap of the clerestory windows, and the double columns with their trapped sills on the parish hall elevation all suggest the possibility of seven bays. The nine bays of the portico, the nine scrunches in the gallery ceilings (see Fig. 23), and the second set of columns on the side wall of the parish hall indicate that the building has been compressed and was once nine bays wide. (Fig. 25)

Fig. 24

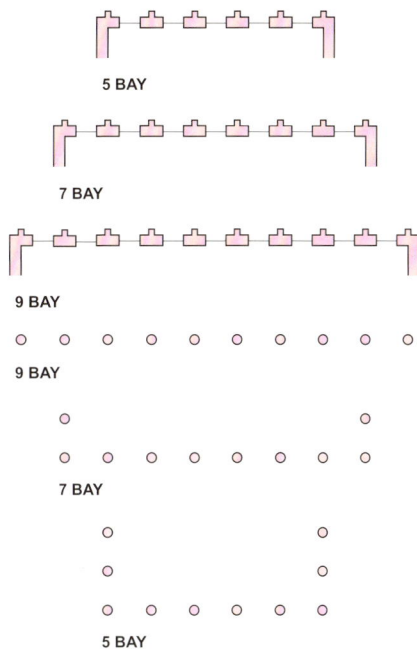

Fig. 25

On the south-north axis, the gabled roofs of the portico, center hall, and parish hall can be understood as an *A-B-A** arrangement. There are at least two overlapping five-bay configurations. Removing the church elements (tower, nave, apse, and galleries) leaves five thin-walled temple bays. (Fig. 26) An actual dimensional square is possible by reconnecting the gallery pavilions to the nave. The niche, the two windows in the apse, and the Palladian window above all suggest that the apse is the result of compressing the three bays. (Figs. 27 & 28) Understanding the center space as temple, the addition of the two-bay portico and the one-bay parish hall makes for seven bays. (Fig. 29) Understanding the central space as the two-bay nave of the church, the two-bay portico, the two-bay nave, the two side aisles, and two gallery pavilions plus the parish bay make for nine bays (Fig. 30).

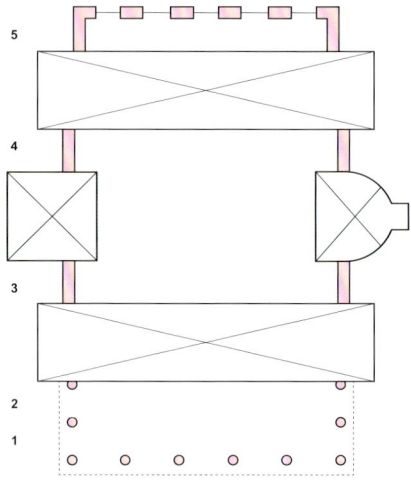

Fig. 26

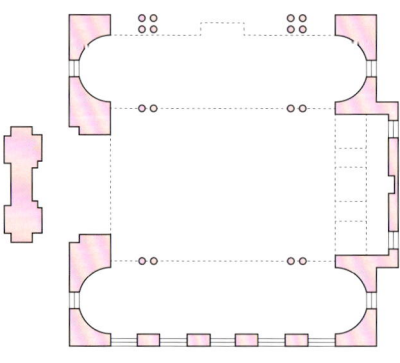

Fig. 27

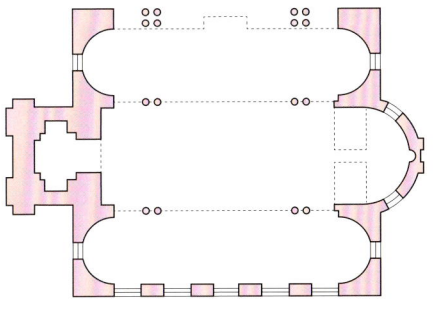

Fig. 28

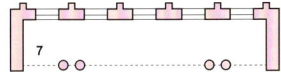

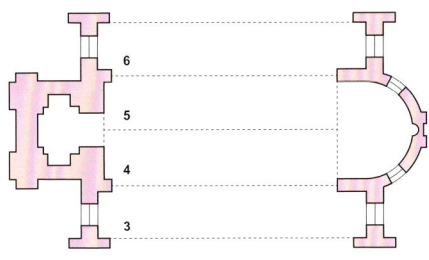

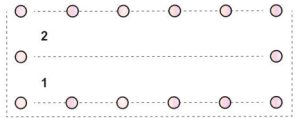

Fig. 29

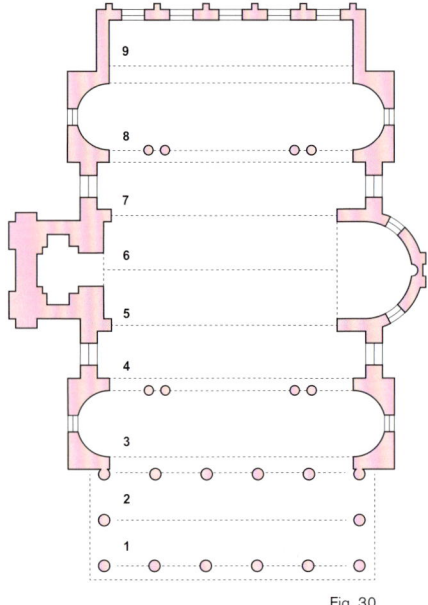

Fig. 30

The dissonance between these various bay structures reinforces the difference between St. George's typological roots in the forms of both temple and church. Of course, temples come in all forms including square, but the most common organization is an odd number of bays on the short end and double that number on the long side. Thus, the five-bay temple front would require ten bays along the north-south axis. This is easily achieved by considering the apse with its niche and two windows to be three bays arrayed along a curve. However, if we consider the apse to be two bays wide, it is possible to achieve ten bays by spreading the columns between the gallery and parish hall, thereby adding a bay to the parish hall and making it symmetrical with the portico. (Fig. 31) Such a reading is triggered by the double columns between the parish hall and the gallery, which suggest that a missing bay lies between.

The steeple announces the temple-church in the sky. Formed of classical elements, it has all the characteristics of the church. It is composed of discrete pieces and is vertical, compressed, thick-walled, and heavily arched on the lower half. The reference elements are clear: an exaggerated triumphal arch, a treasury, a stepped pyramid, a Roman altar, and the statue of George I. One could read the steeple as a denser version of the Sacred Way at Delphi, with George standing in for Apollo. However, there is also an equivalence between four of the pieces: the base, triumphal arch, treasury, and stepped pyramid are all the same height. George standing on the altar is half the height of the other elements. (Figs. 32 & 33)

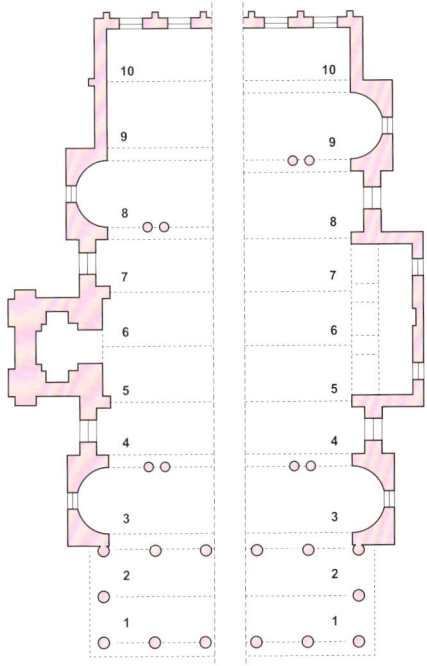

Fig. 31

Fig. 32

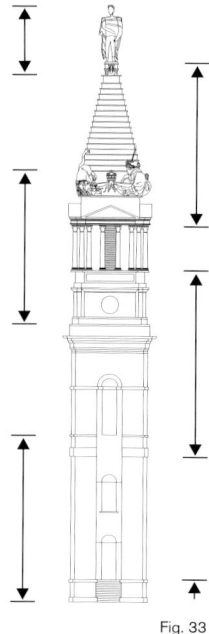

Fig. 33

The tower is completely disproportionate with respect to the building. (Fig. 34) It is possible to excuse this exaggeration as compensation for the church's entrance being removed from the street. But for all its height, the steeple is also compressed. Each of the elements overlaps those above and below. George is joined with the altar that is matched with a finial on top of the stepped pyramid. The base of the pyramid is the attic of the treasury and—so there isn't any confusion about the joining—the lion and unicorn are used like staples to hold the two together. The base of the treasury is the attic of the triumphal arch. Finally, there is the overlap of the triumphal arch and its vertical extension. To press another metaphor into use: the attics and bases are the knots that hold the pearls on the string. They are both a more sophisticated version of the modernist reveal and a representation of the compression manifested throughout the church building. (see Fig. 33)

In addition to the vertical compaction, the entire tower is pressed into the central hall and registers internal compressions in plan. In keeping with the compression of the church on the west-east axis, the east and west elevations of the triumphal arch and its extruded base have been flattened. The flattening is expressed in both the disproportionate height and recesses of the arches. The result is that in the treasury there is too much material in too little space as indicated by the odd diagonal columns at the corners, which appear to have been squeezed out of the otherwise orthogonal organization. (Fig. 35)

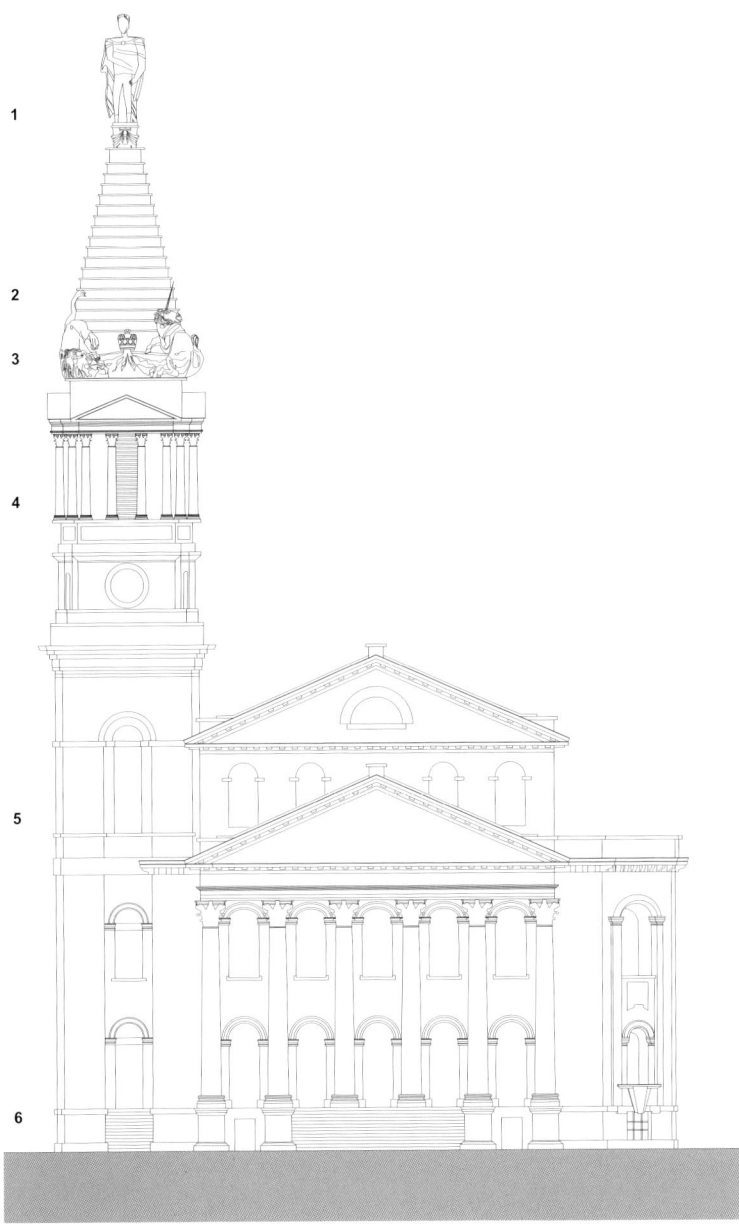

1. ST. GEORGE 2. PYRAMID 3. LION & UNICORN 4. TREASURY 5. TRIUMPHAL ARCH 6. BASE

Fig. 34

Fig. 35

The development of the thick walls and arches is rather ingenious. At ground level, the deep arched recesses on the north and south elevations begin the procession to doop arches that concludes at the church's apse. In the vertical dimension, that thickness is enhanced in the triumphal arch, its attic, the stepped pyramid, and the sacrificial altar, all of which might be taken as solid. Considering the cornices of the triumphal arch and the temple-church while understanding how disparate pieces are tied together elsewhere in the building, it is easy to consider a scenario where the two were once aligned and that the triumphal arch has been pushed up to the roof. (Figs. 36 & 37) This understanding makes sense of the columns in the treasury, which become the spacers between the church and its former reasonably-scaled tower while marking the pop-up of the center pavilion. These moves reinforce the vertical reading of the church by leaving the two-story piers unencumbered at the main floor.

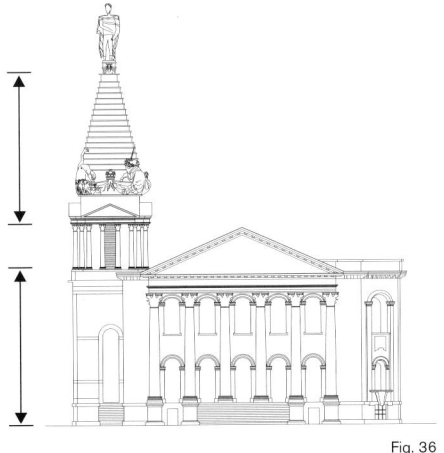

Fig. 36

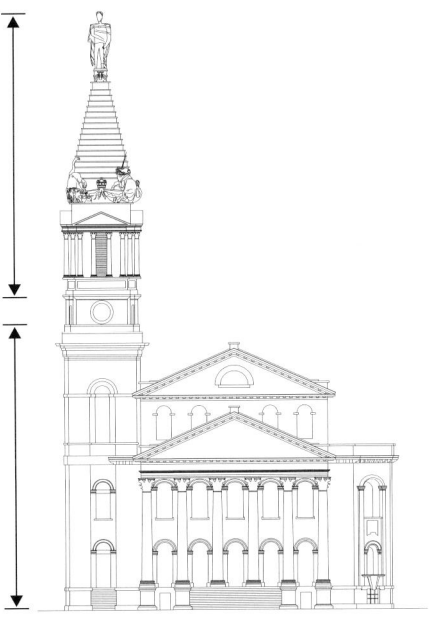

Fig. 37

For all of the ambiguity in its relationships with site and self, St. George's Bloomsbury is a strikingly coherent whole. What began as a rough skewering of temple-to-church ends up as a marriage of two complementary forms. Each retains—and indeed enhances—its respective identity in a remarkable compositional dance that involves absorbing the qualities and experiences of the other.

CREDITS

All reasonable efforts have been made to identify and contact the copyright holders of the visual material reproduced in this book. The publisher and the Knowlton School of Architecture apologize to anyone who has not been reached or properly credited. Errors and omissions should be brought to our attention and will be corrected in future editions.

SIMILARITY AND DIFFERENCE: SANAA'S GRACE FARMS RIVER BUILDING
Fig. 1 Photo by Iwan Baan
Fig. 12 Photo by Dean Kaufman
Fig. 22 Photo by Iwan Baan

SHOEHORNING THE SITE: KOOLHAAS' VILLA DALL'AVA
Fig. 1 Photo by Ernest Delaville. Licensed under the Attribution 2.0 Generic (CC BY 2.0) license
Fig. 5 Photo by Hans Werlemann, courtesy of OMA
Fig. 6 © Peter Aaron/OTTO
Fig. 8 © Peter Aaron/OTTO
Fig. 10 © Peter Aaron/OTTO
Fig. 12 © Peter Aaron/OTTO
Fig. 16 © Peter Aaron/OTTO
Fig. 23 Photo by Hans Werlemann, courtesy of OMA
Fig. 25 Photo by Hans Werlemann, courtesy of OMA
Fig. 26 © Peter Aaron/OTTO

AS A CONSEQUENCE: STIRLING'S NEUE STAATSGALERIE
Fig. 3 James Stirling/Michael Wilford fonds. Canadian Centre for Architecture
Fig. 5 James Stirling/Michael Wilford fonds. Canadian Centre for Architecture
Fig. 8 James Stirling/Michael Wilford fonds. Canadian Centre for Architecture
Fig. 14 *2018-05-FL-184981* by ACME london. Licensed under Creative Commons Attribution-NonCommercial 2.0 Generic (CC BY-NC 2.0) license (https://creativecommons.org/licenses/by-nc/2.0/)
Fig. 21 James Stirling/Michael Wilford fonds. Canadian Centre for Architecture
Fig. 22 Photo by de:Benutzer:Mussklprozz. Licensed under the Creative Commons Attribution-Share Alike 3.0 Unported license
Fig. 25 Photo by Fred Romero. Licensed under the Creative Commons Attribution 2.0 Generic license
Fig. 27 imageBROKER / Alamy Stock Photo
Fig. 29 James Stirling/Michael Wilford fonds. Canadian Centre for Architecture
Fig. 30 imageBROKER / Alamy Stock Photo
Fig. 32 Photo by Fred Romero. Photo has been cropped. Licensed under the Creative Commons Attribution 2.0 Generic license
Fig. 34 Photo by Immanuel Giel. Licensed under the Creative Commons Attribution-Share Alike 4.0 International license
Fig. 36 Photo by Jairmsilva. Licensed under the Creative Commons Attribution-Share Alike 4.0 International license
Fig. 37 James Stirling/Michael Wilford fonds. Canadian Centre for Architecture
Fig. 40 Staatsgalerie Stuttgart Stuttgart, Germany View of the theater arch from below, 1978. Graphite and color pencil on tracing paper. 23 3/8 x 19 7/8" (59.4 x 50.5 cm). Gift of the architect. Digital Image © The Museum of Modern Art/Licensed by SCALA / Art Resource, NY
Fig. 43 James Stirling/Michael Wilford fonds. Canadian Centre for Architecture
Fig. 44 Photo by Andrea Welz, Stuttgart (kunstundreisen.com)

PILING IT ON: VANNA VENTURI HOUSE
Fig. 17 Photo by Rollin LaFrance, The Architectural Archives, University of Pennsylvania by the gift of Robert Venturi and Denise Scott Brown
Fig. 28 © Bill Maris /Esto
Fig. 29 © Bill Maris /Esto
Fig. 31 Photo by Rollin LaFrance, courtesy of Venturi, Scott Brown and Associates

PRIMORDIAL PRESENCE: KAHN'S KIMBELL ART MUSEUM
Fig. 2 Photo by Peter J. Sieger
Fig. 3 Photo by Peter J. Sieger
Fig. 6 Photo by Jeff Stvan - FOR[A] Photography
Fig. 17 ©Nic Lehoux
Fig. 21 Photo by Mary Ann Sullivan
Fig. 23 *The Kimbell Art Museum in Fort Worth, Texas (United States)* by Michael Barera. Licensed under the Creative Commons Attribution-Share Alike 4.0 International license
Fig. 27 Kimbell Art Museum, Fort Worth, Texas. Constructed 1969–72. South gallery with Pierre Bonnard's Landscape at Le Cannet. Louis I. Kahn (1901–1974), architect. Photograph: Robert LaPrelle. © 2019 Kimbell Art Museum, Fort Worth
Fig. 29 ©Nic Lehoux

WHIRRING BITS: CHAREAU'S MAISON DE VERRE
Fig. 1 Photo by August Fischer. Licensed under the Attribution-NoDerivs 2.0 Generic (CC BY-ND 2.0) license
Fig. 8 Carapetian, Michael (b. 1938). Maison de Verre, Paris. 1966. Gelatin silver print, 9 13/16 x 6 11/16" (25 x 17 cm). Gift of Emilio Ambasz. Digital Image © The Museum of Modern Art/Licensed by SCALA / Art Resource, NY
Fig. 14 Photo by Jean Collas. © MAD, Paris. Location: Paris, musée des Arts décoratifs
Fig. 27 Photo by Michael Carapetian
Fig. 29 Photo by Michael Carapetian
Fig. 33 Photo by Michael Carapetian
Fig. 34 Photo by Jean Collas. © MAD, Paris. Location: Paris, musée des Arts décoratifs

GULP: HAWKSMOOR'S ST. GEORGE'S BLOOMSBURY
Fig. 1 Photo by Angelo Hornak

BIOGRAPHY

Robert S. Livesey is Professor and Director Emeritus at the Knowlton School of Architecture at The Ohio State University. He is the former chair of the Department of Architecture, former director of the Knowlton School of Architecture, former head of the Architecture Section, and former interim head of the Landscape Architecture Section. He has taught at Yale University, the University of Pennsylvania, and Syracuse University.

He has won several teaching awards including the Judith Capen Teaching Award at Yale University, the AIA Ohio Teaching Award, the Alumni Award for Distinguished Teaching at The Ohio State University, and the AIAS Educator Honor Award. In addition, he is an honorary member of the Sphinx Senior Honorary at OSU.

He is a principal of Robert Livesey Architect and has won numerous design awards, including a Citation from Progressive Architecture and American Institute of Architects Honor Awards. His work has been published in national and international journals and been exhibited widely. He has lectured at numerous universities.

He holds an A.B. in Architecture from Princeton University and a Master of Architecture from Harvard University. He is registered to practice architecture in Connecticut and Ohio. In addition to other recognitions, he is a Fellow of the American Institute of Architects and the American Academy in Rome.